THE PHILOSOPHER
AND THE GOSPELS

From the author of
Is Religion Dangerous?
Is Religion Irrational?
More Than Matter: What Humans Really Are
Why There Almost Certainly Is a God

KEITH WARD
THE PHILOSOPHER
AND THE GOSPELS

JESUS THROUGH THE LENS OF PHILOSOPHY

Copyright © 2011 Keith Ward
This edition copyright © 2011 Lion Hudson

The author asserts the moral right
to be identified as the author of this work

A Lion Book
an imprint of
Lion Hudson plc
Wilkinson House, Jordan Hill Road,
Oxford OX2 8DR, England
www.lionhudson.com
ISBN 978 0 7459 5562 9

Distributed by:
UK: Marston Book Services, PO Box 269, Abingdon, Oxon, OX14 4YN
USA: Trafalgar Square Publishing, 814 N. Franklin Street, Chicago, IL 60610
USA Christian Market: Kregel Publications, PO Box 2607, Grand Rapids, Michigan 49501

First edition 2011
10 9 8 7 6 5 4 3 2 1 0

All rights reserved

Acknowledgments
p. 111 Scripture quotation taken from The Revised Standard Version of the Bible copyright
© 1346, 1952 and 1971 by the Division of Christian Education of the National Council of
Churches in the USA. Used by permission. All Rights Reserved.

All other scripture quotations are from The New Revised Standard Version of the Bible
copyright © 1989 by the Division of Christian Education of the National Council of Churches
in the USA. Used by permission. All Rights Reserved.

A catalogue record for this book is available
from the British Library

Typeset in 11.5/14 Venetian 301 BT
Printed and bound in Great Britain MPG Books

Contents

Preface

I owe a great debt to the many people who have helped to shape my thoughts on philosophy, Christian faith and my understanding of the New Testament.

The earliest major influences were Methodist ministers in Northumberland, notably Frank Froude and Gordon Bolderson, who first inspired me both in Christian faith and in critical thinking.

When, at the University of Cardiff, I discovered that there was such a subject as philosophy, Lynn Evans and Humphrey Palmer guided me towards thinking of academic life.

At Oxford, my tutors, Gilbert Ryle and Geoffrey Warnock, forced me to think even harder, and Ian Ramsey (later Bishop of Durham) convinced me of the moral and intellectual rigour of Christian faith.

When I later taught philosophy at King's College, London, Christopher Evans and Leslie Houlden imbued me with a love for the New Testament, together with an admiration for the work of modern biblical scholars.

Later still, back at Oxford, the New Testament scholar Robert Morgan was amazingly generous with his time and energy, reading the whole manuscript of this book and making it very much better by his comments, which seemed to be always exactly right, and to correct some of my aged exuberances. It is to him, in particular, that I owe my gratitude for making this book what it is – while exempting him from responsibility for the wilder things I say. I was particularly moved by his fairly frequent comment "Oh!", written in the margin, which always warned me that something was wrong.

Finally, my wife Marian has always endured my long periods of absence in my study and has inspired me with a life that wonderfully exemplifies what I often boringly preach.

To all these, and to the many others who go unmentioned, I give thanks, hoping that they would maybe even be a little pleased, or at least (thinking especially, perhaps, of Gilbert Ryle) not too embarrassed by the influence they have had.

Part 1
Approaching the Gospels

What can a philosopher say about the Gospels?

I began this book by wanting to look at the Gospels as a philosopher, and see what emerged. In particular, I looked at the "Sermon on the Mount" (Matthew 5–7) and at the parables in the first three (Synoptic) Gospels, because they claimed to give the teachings of Jesus. Accordingly, I did not look at the miracles, the healing ministry, or the passion of Jesus, even though these are major themes in the Gospels. I wanted to concentrate on how the Gospel writers had presented the teachings of Jesus.

When I did this, three themes leaped from the pages of the Synoptic Gospels. It seemed to me that Jesus' teaching was, above all, that God was a God of limitless and self-giving love. There are some passages in Jesus' parables that seem to stress God's terrible judgment and God's exclusion of sinners from salvation. Clearly, this is a problem. Being a philosopher, I set out to explore the idea of a God of unconditional love and its implications, and to see if there was a way of interpreting the parables of judgment and exclusion that was consistent with such an idea. My first theme was in place, that the Christian gospel is one of universal salvation. Some theologians call this *conditional universalism*, because it says that everyone can be saved, but does not logically entail that everyone will be saved.

Then there are some parables that speak of the "end of the age", of the judgment of God on the nations, and some that speak of the choosing of an "elect" people. These, too, seem very problematic, on two main counts. First, they seem to suggest that God only really loves a few people of faith, and leaves the rest to a terrible fate. Second, the world did not end within the first generation of believers, as a number of verses apparently say it should have done. The main problem here is one of interpretation. What do terms like the "Son of man" or his coming on "clouds of glory with angels" really mean? Can they be taken literally, or do they have a symbolic meaning, referring to real events, but not in a literal way? Here again a philosopher may have something to say, both about the nature of metaphorical or symbolic speech in general, and about how we can use language as a very inadequate vehicle to speak of the relation between an eternal and infinite God and a temporal and finite creation. This led me to the idea that Jesus was speaking of profound truths, but they are spiritual truths about the world to come, not literal truths about this physical world. And that seemed to me to make a great deal of sense of some of the most difficult parts of the New Testament. I have called this a *spiritual eschatology*, because it teaches that there is a future in which evil will be eliminated and Christ will rule (that is "eschatology", the doctrine of the "last things" or the ultimate destiny of the whole creation). But it is not a future in this physical world. Rather, it is a future in the world to come, the "new creation" that is promised in the New Testament.

Finally, many parables seem to be about life in the kingdom of God. In modern moral philosophy, there is a great interest in what is called "virtue ethics". Attention is not concentrated on moral rules or on ways of obtaining the greatest happiness of the greatest number (often called deontology and consequentialism, respectively). The focus is on what sort of person one should be, on the virtues or excellences of character that go to form a good person. Looking at many of the parables in this light, a good account can be given of them by seeing them as portraying the sort of virtues that we would have if we saw Jesus as our moral ideal, and if we sought to let the Spirit of God form in us the virtues that were fully actual in Jesus.

True religion is, a philosopher may say (at least this one would), a matter of practice. It is a discipline of the soul by which liberation is sought from egoism, pride, and hatred, and union is sought with the beauty and perfection of God. So Christian morality will be closely bound up with a spiritual discipline of the soul, and with belief in a God who, Christians believe, can bring the soul by the power of the Spirit to share in the life of Christ. Philosophers might call this a *participative virtue ethics*, because it sees the excellences of mind and character at which humans should aim as responses to, and participation in, the nature of God as revealed in Jesus.

When these three themes emerged, I decided to develop them by putting down in italics my own versions of the "Sermon on the Mount" and virtually all the recorded parables of Jesus. Then I wrote a sort of personal commentary on them, so that readers can see how my three main themes grew as I read the recorded teachings of Jesus. When I say "my own versions", what I mean is that they are not translations. They are expressions of what they meant to me as I read them. I have tried not actually to falsify them, and hope that they are plausible readings. But I know that the parables will mean different things to different people, and I am not claiming that these are the "correct" or "real" meanings of the parables. I think that my three main themes are reasonable readings of the Gospel material, but they do not wholly depend upon the small summaries of the parables that I give in the italicized passages. Let those summaries just be reminders of the parables and indicators of one personal response to them.

These three themes spring from a reading of the "Sermon on the Mount" and the parables in the Synoptic Gospels. The fourth Gospel is significantly different, containing no parables and only one (double) mention of the kingdom of God (John 3:3, 5). We need to account for this difference, and New Testament scholars have done that. What a philosopher can do is to ask if a general philosophical worldview can be found in John's Gospel, and if so, what it is. That is precisely what, as my fourth theme, I try to do.

I conclude that the Gospel of John, and to some extent the non-canonical Gospel of Thomas, suggests a total theistic worldview that is only implicit in the Synoptic Gospels. John's doctrine of the mutual indwelling of Jesus and "God the Father", together with the teaching of the unity of believers "in Christ" (especially in the parable of the vine in John 15), naturally led to what was later unfolded in patristic theology as the union of the human and divine natures in Christ. But, in a way that would surprise some Christians, I will argue that it even more naturally lends support to the formulation of an idealist metaphysics, a *unitive idealism*. Idealism is a philosophical system which postulates that mind, or at least something mind-like, is the ultimate reality of which the whole material universe is an expression or appearance. That, of course, for Christians, is God. Idealism is unitive if it claims that the universe, which may be estranged or alienated from its underlying source of being, has the ultimate goal of being united to Absolute Mind.

In its Christian form, it asserts that the being of the eternal God is temporally expressed in creation and redemption – and here John's image of the "Word" becoming flesh is paradigmatic. God then brings the whole temporal creation to participate in the divine being as its completion and consummation – and that, I suggest, is the implication of the teachings that Jesus is the saviour of the world (John 1:29), and that the redeemed are "in" Christ, who is "in" the Father. John's Gospel can be read as suggesting that there is in the teaching of Jesus just such an idealist metaphysic, though Jesus himself expressed it in the symbolic forms of Jewish imagery that are found in the Synoptic Gospels.

If the Gospel of John is an authentic unfolding of themes implicit in the Synoptic Gospels, then it becomes plausible to hold that Jesus might have somehow envisaged the goal of a union of humanity with the divine, which was foreshadowed and actualized in his own person. It then becomes much more plausible to believe that Jesus was aware of his unique identity with God, and this will influence any assessment of what his teaching was. It becomes more probable, other things being equal, that Jesus himself taught that God's love is universal; that he used language about the "end of the age" in a symbolic, not literal, way; that he taught a spiritual way of overcoming egoism and participating in the life of God through the indwelling of the Spirit; and that he taught that the fulfilment of such participation, however exactly it may come about, is the final goal of human life.

Some would say, however, that all we can know is that these teachings existed in early Christian traditions which arose from reflection on Jesus' life and death. In that case, we must, if we are Christian disciples, at least say that such traditions do not fundamentally mistake the implications of Jesus' own teaching, and that we do not worship a Jesus who never existed, or who would have denied these traditions. Allowing that possibility, I will nevertheless sometimes refer to these traditions as "Jesus' teachings", meaning that they are teachings I think Jesus is likely to have given, or that were implicit in and consonant with what he did teach.

There are, of course, other interpretations of Jesus' teaching than this. But I suspect that it is a lack of philosophical reflection on biblical language and belief that has sometimes led to some over-literal and spiritually superficial interpretations that seem to be widespread today. It is also true that historical Jesus research has usually been more interested in relating Jesus to his first-century Jewish environment than to the impact of his life and teaching on subsequent believers. The philosopher may be guided by an interest in the moral and metaphysical beliefs which seem to be implied by the recorded Gospel teachings. Sometimes those implications have taken centuries to be made explicit – for instance, the realization that slavery and sexual inequality are incompatible with the Gospel teaching took almost 2,000 years to become widespread!

The philosopher deals in questions of meaning and interpretation, in different possible ways of reading the Gospel texts, perhaps for different purposes. The Gospels are, after all, not just historical memoirs. They are written for a purpose – to proclaim Jesus as the messiah (in the Synoptic Gospels) or as the "saviour of the world" (in John's Gospel). They are written to sustain and develop the faith of communities of disciples of Jesus, who already believed that, as Paul put it, "Christ died for our sins in accordance with the scriptures, and that he was buried, and that he was raised on the third day" (1 Corinthians 15:3–4).

Christian churches today still hold that basic belief, and they take the Gospels as canonical texts which are to be used for sustaining and developing faith in a very different world from that of Jesus' time. The philosophical theologian is interested in how the texts can be read to do that job. The interest is mainly about how the records of Jesus' teachings can be used in developing a living Christian faith today.

There must of course be some connection between what Jesus actually said and a specific modern interpretation of ancient texts. Throughout the ages, different interpretations of his recorded teachings, often arising within different church traditions, may be seen as sometimes more and sometimes less natural and plausible developments of his teachings. Contemporary Christian views arise out of centuries of worship of the risen Christ, of thinking over what such worship implies about Jesus' unique status as an object of worship, and of general ideas about God, human destiny, and the nature of revelation, that have been partly developed in response to advances in human knowledge, and that have been formed, often after protracted arguments, in specific historical traditions of worship.

It could be that Jesus shows the nature of God and God's purpose, without consciously moving beyond the perspective of a first-century Palestinian Jew who was concerned to obey God's will and proclaim God's coming kingdom to his fellow Jews. As the church grew in the Gentile world, it developed more universal ideas of the kingdom and interpreted memories of the life of Jesus in the light of the resurrection appearances to the disciples. That process of development has continued for 2,000 years through many different cultures and philosophies. Our reading of the texts today will probably differ from that of the original writers.

The philosopher will be interested in the question of how the original teachings, in the light of all the scholarly disputes about what those may have been, can be seen as containing basic themes and latent possibilities of development that will make it reasonable to see Jesus as the source and inspiration of a specific interpretation of modern Christian teachings, as well as the proper object of Christian worship.

I have found Jesus' recorded teachings to be philosophically profound, far more than good stories with a nice moral attached or clear instructions that need little thought to understand and put into practice. Such profundity, in my view, suggests a source, not in groups of argumentative disciples, but in a spiritual teacher of unique knowledge and insight. What has impressed me more and more as I have read the Gospels is the transcendent mystery of Christ and the ever-elusive yet always illuminating character of his teaching. This book tries to convey that – but I have no hope of putting as simply as he did thoughts that are as profound as his.

Can we know what Jesus taught?

I am very conscious of the fact that I am not a New Testament scholar, and I depend almost entirely on the historical, linguistic, and cultural researches of those who are. I am writing as a philosopher who uses such research as a resource, but whose primary focus is the text as it stands in the New Testament. I think that no serious student of the Bible can afford to neglect the work of the best biblical scholars. But contemporary scholarship leads to vastly different portraits of Jesus, with no obvious way of arbitrating between them. Sometimes decisions between conflicting scholarly interpretations have to be made, and I have tried to note where I have made them and why. On the whole, I am not claiming that I know Jesus thought this way. My claim is that we can, as disciples of Jesus, read the recorded responses to Jesus that we find in the Gospels in this way. The implication is that this is an intelligible development from Jesus' teaching, even if it is not an exact reproduction of it.

First I need to address some general questions about how the recorded teachings of Jesus relate to what the historical Jesus might have taught, and how they may have been influenced by factors arising in the life of the early churches. This is not first-order historical Jesus research on my part, but a philosophical reflection on the principles and presuppositions underlying such research. This will give a basis upon which my philosophical and theological interpretation of the Gospels may proceed.

All biblical scholars are well aware that pure historical research can give no certainty about what Jesus taught. Our pictures of Jesus are at least in part reflections of our own ideals of what a great spiritual teacher should be (or maybe, in some cases, reflections of a belief that religion is an illusion and there is no God). Some views, however, are generally thought to be more plausible than others. In assessing historical documents of this sort, three main sets of considerations are relevant. First there is the question of general worldview. If you believe there is no God, or that Jesus was a mistaken prophet of the end of the world, you will seek an interpretation for which Jesus was at best, as Geza Vermes holds, a Galilean holy man or *Hasid* – not a scholar, but a rural miracle-worker and exorcist who met a tragic and untimely end. If, on the other hand, you believe that there is a God and that God created the cosmos for the sake of good, you may be more disposed to see Jesus as (at least) a prophet inspired by God, who may indeed have appeared after his death to his disciples. Assessments of the wisdom and worth of Jesus' recorded teachings will be affected by such background worldviews.

Second, there is the question of whether you accept, on grounds of faith, the authority of some church tradition or not. If you do, you may well think that the recorded teachings of Jesus are authentic, at least in general. You will think that the church has been right in believing, for instance, that Jesus is the human image and act of God. If so, Jesus' own beliefs may have been culturally restricted (for example, he would not have known about the size or age of the cosmos), but he did have unique knowledge of the nature and reality of God, and of the right way to relate to God. His recorded teachings may have been developed in slightly different ways by the Gospel editors, but they have not been completely changed either by the early church or by Paul, as Vermes and Crossan seem to suggest. They will be consistent with his being the saviour who is presently experienced in the community of your church.

If you are a convinced atheist, you will be disposed to think that Jesus and the traditions arising from him were pretty basically mistaken in some fundamental matters. Or if you belong to a more liberal church tradition, you may think that the recorded teachings are sayings arising within the early churches to meet their own specific spiritual needs, and that it does not matter so much whether they go back to a historical Jesus. Different churches take differing views on these matters. My point is merely that it would be reasonable to let your commitment to a particular church tradition influence your evaluation of the historical evidence. In short, it is a matter of faith that the Christ of faith is, or is an authentic development of, the Jesus of history. Such faith is not blind. It is a reasonable reading of a historical figure that cannot be objectively and conclusively verified, but that is strongly implied by present commitment to a tradition that claims to be derived from him. For present-day disciples of Jesus, he is the matrix or reliable foundation of a developing and diverse set of traditions which claim to disclose the divine nature and purpose. If you belong to or sympathize with one of these traditions, it will be reasonable for your historical judgments to be influenced (but, of course, neither overruled nor completely determined) by that fact.

Third, there is the question of assigning Jesus a plausible place in the history and culture of Galilee in the times of Pontius Pilate. Knowledge of the Aramaic language, the imagery of Apocalyptic, and messianic claimants before the Jewish War will give Jesus a historical context that will help in interpreting what his recorded teachings may have meant. Views on these matters will be important in deciding, for instance, whether Jesus could have claimed to be the messiah, whether he could have used "Son of man" as a title (Vermes claims that it was not possible to do so), and what he meant by the kingdom of God.

One method used by some New Testament scholars to establish which of Jesus' reported teachings are likely to be genuine is the criterion of dissimilarity. Professor Crossan writes that "a rigorous negativity must be invoked to separate what Jesus said or did from what the tradition records".[1] If any reported sayings of Jesus can be found in contemporaneous Jewish records, or if they express known general attitudes of the primitive church, they must be rejected. This means that the only authentic sayings of Jesus will be those that differ from the views of his Jewish contemporaries and from those of the early church.

It is now widely agreed that this is an unduly restrictive criterion, since few people can be wholly original in everything they say, and it is to be hoped that few teachers are almost totally misunderstood by their disciples, if they have any. It seems much more likely that Jesus would largely share the views of his culture, even if he interpreted them in an original way, and that his disciples would at least grasp the main gist of what he taught, even if they drew some inferences that were suspect.

It is plausible to say that we might be most certain of statements that seem to be unique to Jesus, since it is hard to see any other source for them. But it is not so plausible to dismiss as unreliable statements ascribed to Jesus that have parallels in Jewish or early Christian thought.

On the contrary, I would have thought they might have a high likelihood of being authentic. Indeed Geza Vermes proposes a view of Jesus which he thinks probable precisely because it is more like Galilean thought of the time than unlike it. With regard to early Christian thought, N.T. Wright plausibly thinks that the unanimous New Testament belief that Jesus was the messiah, together with the church's experience of the risen Lord as a decisive revelation of God, raises the probability that Jesus in some sense made that claim. It was obviously possible for a Jew to make such a claim, since there were other messianic claimants around at the time, even though Jesus' interpretation of the messianic kingdom was unlike that of most other messianic claimants, in being apparently non-political and non-violent. In both these cases, it is the similarity of Jesus' claims to those of Jewish and early Christian thought that raises the probability of his recorded teachings being authentic.

Other factors than dissimilarity or similarity are important in assessing what Jesus may have said. I think the most important is the writer's view of what a great spiritual teacher must have been like. Thus John Dominic Crossan is attracted to cryptic teachings which express a profound spiritual experience, while Marcus Borg actually says, "I don't want Jesus to have seen his own death as having the significance Tom [Wright] gives to it", and "if you think you are the light of the world, you're not".[2] These are honest statements of opinion. But I think that a saint could easily see his or her death as an act of obedience to God that might be spiritually significant and have a positive part to play in the realization of God's purposes. And many saints in many religious traditions have in some sense identified themselves with God, without being completely crazy. If Jesus was the light of the world, I even think it would be rather odd if he had no inkling of the fact. So, while I admire Marcus Borg's general approach to Jesus, I differ from him in what he thinks a spiritual teacher (especially one who was Jewish) might be expected to believe about himself.

It seems to me that the most plausible line to take is that Jesus probably said things that were common in the Jewish culture in which he was raised, but he must have given a significant and memorable dramatic twist to them so that the genesis of early church worship of Jesus was not an exaggerated or irrational response to the memory of his life and teaching. A criterion of dissimilarity does not quite catch that.

The other main criteria that have been used to try to establish the authentic teaching of Jesus – sorting out which New Testament writings are likely to be earliest, being impressed by independent attestations from more than one source ("multiple attestation"), and accepting sayings and interpretations that cohere and are consistent with other interpretations that you are inclined to accept, are valuable and important. But it must be remembered that while these may increase the probability that some teachings are authentic, they do not decrease the probability that many other teachings (like those in the Gospel of John, for example), while undoubtedly later and theory-laden, may be authentic interpretations of the partly hidden meaning of Jesus' teachings.

In no case will there be certainty beyond reasonable doubt. This truth should make Christians tolerant of a range of diverse interpretations of the person of Jesus – from Marcus Borg to Tom Wright – since all must admit that different people will weigh the probabilities differently, yet all Christians may see Christ as a definitive disclosure of the saving will of God. The Christian church cannot without wilful blindness insist on one sole interpretation of Christian truth.

We must all live with diversity, probability, and doubt. We Christians cannot escape this by refraining from coming to decisions about Jesus, and trying just to have some sort of minimal belief in God. For even a minimal belief in God is far from being a certainty beyond reasonable doubt. Some people believe that there is some sort of God, and other people believe that there is no God, in similar conditions of objective uncertainty. That is just the human condition. All beliefs about Jesus – even the belief that he existed at all – are going to be based on assessments of probability. We must frankly accept that, and hold by the view that seems most probable to us, after reasonably informed enquiry.

The probability that Jesus never existed is very small, whereas the probability that he had disciples, taught in Galilee, was a healer and exorcist, and was crucified, is very great. There will still, however, be unresolvable differences in assessments of probability. For instance, I believe in God. I believe that God is a loving God who desires the salvation of all finite creatures. I believe that I encounter God under the description of the living Christ in the community of the church. And I believe that Jesus' recorded teachings are of unmistakeably personal and uniquely wise spiritual depth. In consequence, I am able to assign a high probability to the disciples' claims that Jesus was in some sense raised from death. But someone who lacked all these prior beliefs might think the resurrection highly improbable and would have to assess the records of Jesus' life accordingly.

I am also liable to think that the moral teaching of Jesus is much more important than whatever eschatological beliefs he may have had. For that moral teaching remains relevant to Christian discipleship in every age, whereas, as Albert Schweitzer said, the particular eschatological beliefs of first-century Judaism have become matters of mainly historical and antiquarian interest. Furthermore, while it is possible, and even likely, that Jesus' teaching was almost entirely centred on Israel, the implications of that teaching for a largely Gentile and global church are undoubtedly of universal significance. So I will be led to an interpretation of the Gospel records that downplays any literal interpretations of Jesus' eschatology and that highlights more universal implications of his moral and spiritual teachings.

I do not have these prior beliefs about the nature of the God encountered in Jesus because I invented them on my own, without any knowledge of Christian belief, and was then determined to impose them on the Gospels. Maybe I would believe in God whether or not I was a Christian. But it could be that I might not even have the concept of God if I had not known something about Christianity, or at least about other theistic religions. So even my prior beliefs are influenced by religion, as they are influenced by all the other knowledge I have been taught during my life.

The important thing is to acknowledge the many diverse and often conflicting influences upon our beliefs, and accept that we have to try to make informed commitments in situations of objective uncertainty. We can rank many of our own beliefs by degrees of probability, and such rankings are likely to reflect the practical difference they make to our lives, rather than some dispassionate measure of a quasi-statistical sort.

When considering the teachings of Jesus, I consider it highly probable that he taught love of enemies and the importance of forgiveness, and not very probable, in fact quite unlikely, that he taught the existence of endless hell. That is because – looking at the three sets of considerations mentioned just now – my worldview conceives God as creating for the sake of good, not harm. My spiritual experience is of God as compassionate and merciful, not tyrannical and severe. And my knowledge of the Judaism of Jesus' time, and of the figurative nature of much of Jesus' language, leads me to a non-literal understanding of the metaphors in the New Testament which later led to the development of a doctrine of hell.

These considerations – worldview, experience, historical knowledge, and analysis of linguistic forms – all converge on a specific interpretation of Jesus' teachings. I know any interpretation will not be universal or overwhelmingly compelling. But I can say that I find a specific interpretation reasonable and most probable, given my prior beliefs, which themselves have been formed by many influences, including but not limited to influences from various Christian churches.

Bearing all this in mind, I would wish to take seriously the critical work of scholars like Geza Vermes who do not share my Christian faith, but who know much more about Judaism at the time of Jesus than I do. But I almost certainly will not accept Geza's assumption that Jesus did not really rise from the dead, his belief that Paul virtually started a new religion which had little in common with the beliefs of Jesus, and his belief that the Christian church is not a reliable source of authentic divine revelation. I am open to the possibility that his arguments may force me to change my mind (I have changed my mind about Jesus in the past, moving from atheism to Christian faith). But they would have to be overwhelmingly strong, since they call in question most of my general beliefs about God and my commitment to the church. That does not mean that I am more prejudiced than he is. It just means that my initial background beliefs are just about as prejudiced as his – they have been learned and developed through a lifetime of reading, research, and personal experience.

It is vital to see that no one is without prejudice (this is a term made popular in philosophy by Hans-Georg Gadamer, but perhaps a better word than "prejudice" in English would be "presupposition"), without an initial set of background beliefs which will shape a general interpretation of the evidence. A reasonable investigation will be open to all available relevant evidence and listen to as many arguments as possible in favour of differing specific interpretations of this evidence, and then modify initial views in the light of that process. Initial views of a general nature are unlikely to change completely, though they may do. But it is highly likely that specific beliefs will change considerably as a result of this process. Thus I am not now likely to change my belief that Jesus was raised by God from death, and that the Spirit, working in the church, does bring life, light, joy, and fulfilment to human lives. That means I am unlikely to think that Jesus was just a Galilean holy man, as Geza Vermes does. But my view of Jesus has been greatly affected by what Geza Vermes, Dominic Crossan, and Marcus Borg have written about Jesus' circumstances, and his linguistic and cultural background in a small rural province of the Roman Empire.

I am interested in discovering how to interpret the Gospel texts as we have them, on the assumption that they give a generally reliable account of Jesus' teachings. Modern scholarship has added much to our knowledge of Jesus' context, and of the differing editorial concerns of the compilers of the Gospels, and this is bound to affect any view of what Jesus taught. The view I have depends wholly on the original research of others, though I have had to try to make informed choices where scholars disagree, after having followed the arguments as sympathetically and fully as I can.

My general conclusion is that the Gospels contain various different ways of understanding Jesus, sometimes in tension with one another. But there is one dominant strand, one way of understanding the teaching of Jesus, which runs like a golden thread through the Gospel narratives as we now have them. It is that "God is love, and those who abide in love abide in God, and God abides in them" (1 John 4:16). My aim is to defend the centrality of this understanding, and to show its plausibility, consistency, and applicability to the everyday life of Christian disciples.

The positive gospel

Although this book aims to be a philosophical analysis and reflection on the Gospels, that does not mean that it is neutral on the question of Christian belief. All philosophers have a worldview, a set of basic beliefs that will inevitably show in their thinking, even if it is not explicitly stated. It is only honest to state what this worldview is clearly at the outset, in the knowledge that no one has what the American philosopher Thomas Nagel has called a "view from nowhere". My basic belief, which I shall seek to amplify and substantiate in this book, is simple. It is that what Jesus taught is good news of the universal love of God, which invites everyone to share in the love, compassion, wisdom, and joy of the divine life. Therefore what the church, the community or many communities of the disciples of Jesus, has to proclaim is the possibility of such a transfigured life for everyone without exception.

The Christian way of life is not primarily a matter of obeying a set of specific rules or laws. It is a matter of cultivating attitudes of the heart, or, better, of allowing the divine Spirit to bring those attitudes to mature expression in Christian lives. The culmination and fulfilment of that process is the entrance into "eternal life", participation in the nature of the eternal God.

That is good news not just for Jews, not just for Christians, not just for the people of the earth, but for the whole of this vast universe, and for whatever intelligent life forms exist in it. If God's love is universal, it is certainly not confined to this planet, and the eternal Christ who is enfleshed in the person of Jesus will make it known in ways we cannot imagine to all created souls throughout the galaxies.

God's love is cosmic and all-embracing, and Christians should rejoice that they see it on this small planet, expressed in the person of Jesus, in his death and resurrection, and (though only ambiguously) in the continuing life of the community of the Spirit of Jesus, the church.

Admittedly there exists a very different interpretation of the gospel, which is hardly good news for the vast majority of the world's population at all. It is that God's judgment will come in wrath upon most of the world, and only a few who call upon the name of Jesus will be saved from that terrible day. Moreover, that judgment will come at any moment, so that there is little time to lose before human history comes to an end. Christian morality is largely fixated on matters relating to sexual conduct, and cares most about keeping rules, but is not greatly concerned with caring for all life on the planet or about seeking justice for the poorest people of the world.

As for the rest of the universe, that is irrelevant. There are 100,000 million stars in our galaxy, and 100,000 million galaxies in the observable universe. But they are all irrelevant, and human beings, on this rather peripheral planet, are the central, perhaps the sole, objects of God's interest in creation. When God ends human history, the whole universe will cease to be – a conclusion that is in stark contradiction to virtually all science teaching in the educated world.

This interpretation of the gospel (which, in all honesty, seems to me rather negative, morally limited, and anti-scientific) is not just wilfully made up. What it does is to take some (not all) texts of the Bible literally, as unchangeable and definitive, as though they were words spoken out of any historical context directly by God to us. But there are many other texts that are ignored, and such literalistic interpretations are unable to provide one consistent form of interpretation that can be applied to all the reported sayings of Jesus. What also have to be ignored are the marked differences of style and content, the different audiences, writers, and contexts of the different books of the Bible. Worst of all, the spiritual, symbolic, and metaphorical character of Jesus' teaching is just not seen, and so Jesus is turned into a severely moralistic and judgmental prophet who was mistaken about the end of the world, instead of the profoundly moral and compassionate spiritual teacher that he was. My chief objection to such interpretations is that they pick out carefully selected parts of the Bible to propound a gospel profoundly different from what I believe to be the gospel of Jesus.

I hope to show that these things are so, and that to take Jesus' teachings literally is to pervert their spiritual content. When he spoke of judgment, as he undoubtedly did, it was not to condemn millions to endless suffering, but to persuade people of the need for repentance. It was rhetorical warning, not literal prediction. When he spoke of the "end of the age", it was not primarily to predict (even if it was partly to expect) that human history would end within a generation, but to say that a new age of the Spirit was dawning, which would be completed at the end of time. When he said that faith could move mountains, it was not to claim that Mount Everest could be moved to California by praying very hard, but to say that real faith in God changes the world by changing human lives. By analysis of the rhetorical, metaphorical, and hyperbolic character of Jesus' recorded teachings, I aim to show that it is impossible to give literal interpretations consistently, and no one ever manages to do so. To find the non-literal or symbolic meaning of Jesus' teachings is one of the most important tasks of the serious reader of the New Testament. What I shall seek to show is that there may be many ways of interpreting the teaching of Jesus, but that the overall tenor of the teachings points clearly to the gospel of universal divine love that most Christians have always rightly seen to be the heart of Christian faith.

Reading the Gospels

Although there are many disputes about what exactly Jesus taught, there are also some fairly wide agreements. We know that Jesus probably taught in Aramaic, that the Gospels are written in Greek, and that there are various later versions of the Gospels (including some which never got into the New Testament) which differ over the exact words ascribed to Jesus. We also know that Jesus never wrote his teachings down, and that we do not possess any manuscripts that can be physically dated to the first few generations of disciples. So it seems pretty certain that we do not have the exact words of Jesus. We have variant records of them, in a different language and in a number of later manuscripts. We assume these manuscripts have earlier, now lost, versions, and that they were collections of sayings remembered or passed on orally from original sources that we do not possess.

Careful comparison of the four Gospels brings out many differences between them. In particular, the first three Gospels present the teaching of Jesus as primarily concerned with the kingdom of heaven (or God), and as given mainly in short parables and cryptic aphorisms. The Gospel of John, however, depicts Jesus as uttering long discourses which do not mention the kingdom of heaven, which contain no parables, which speak instead of "eternal life", and which publicly proclaim Jesus' status as the bread of life, the true vine, and the unique way to the Father. This is such a marked difference that we have to find some satisfactory way to account for it. It seems that Jesus could not at the same time have taught publicly or privately in such very different ways. I shall return to address this point towards the end of the book.

It is thus generally agreed by all who study the Gospels carefully that what we have in the Gospels are edited presentations of the teaching of Jesus which at least in part reflect what the editors and their sources discerned in the person of Jesus. We do not have a collection of the actual words of Jesus, without any changes, translations, or editorial interpretations.

This may seem rather negative, as though we cannot trust what the Gospels say. So it is important to see the positive side to these researches. The most important point is that the word of God, for Christians, is not primarily a book. It is the living person of Jesus. To be more accurate, it is the eternal wisdom of God, which existed before creation, long before Jesus of Nazareth was born. But that word is expressed or embodied in an authentic way in the human Jesus. Jesus expresses the eternal word for us, and his life, death, and resurrection tells us something of huge importance about God's love and purpose.

Paul conveys this message, yet hardly ever refers to any actual words of Jesus.

It is, of course, important that the one who died was the true "image of the invisible God". If so, his teachings must have conveyed the love and purpose of God. Nevertheless, those teachings are not the heart of the

Christian message. It is Jesus' sacrifice on the cross, and his resurrection life, known in the present experience of the church, that is central to faith. For what that tells us is that God's nature is self-sacrificial love, which goes to the furthest lengths to identify with human suffering and to raise human lives to share in the life of God. That is the gospel. It was expressed in the accounts of Jesus' crucifixion and resurrection, witnessed by the apostles, confirmed in the experience of the church, and recorded in the New Testament.

It follows that the New Testament will be regarded by Christians as a generally authentic and reliable record of these events. But it is a record made by a number of human witnesses, passed on orally, and only later written down, in a number of different accounts, reflecting differing viewpoints and experiences.

Christians have not usually thought that God dictated the Bible. The books of the Bible are written in many different styles, at many different times, in different languages (Hebrew, Aramaic, and Greek), and with different points of view.

The Gospels we have are memories of Jesus' acts and teachings, expressing different human perceptions of them and reactions to them. It is quite reasonable to believe that we have generally reliable accounts, but they certainly incorporate later reflections on what those teachings meant to various groups of people. We do not have first-hand exact records of what Jesus said, just as he said things, in the language in which he said them. So while the Gospels may be generally reliable witnesses to the word of God (and I think they are), they are not words actually written by God or by Jesus. They rather record differing human memories of and responses to the person of Jesus.

That tells us two very important things. First, we must not use the Gospels as a textbook of instructions direct from God. We should use them as narratives meant to evoke a sense of the living presence of Jesus. And second, we must not expect exact agreement between the Gospels, or among the disciples of Jesus. We should expect a natural and proper diversity of response and interpretation, and recognize that our theologies are human constructs, and not definitive statements from God.

In the light of this, which is really standard teaching in any first-year college course on the Bible, my own attitude would be to take the Gospels as generally accurate remembrances of many of Jesus' teachings, though edited so as to present Jesus from at least four different perspectives. Some of the teachings may have got modified in the telling, and they may thereby have become even more mysterious than they originally were. But I think the records we have show a distinctive voice of great spiritual depth, and carry reliable impressions of the historical Jesus.

What I want to do is to survey the Gospel records of Jesus' teachings, to bring out what seems to me their spiritual meaning. Though this will obviously be my personal response, not "the" one and only truth, it is intended to be a response to the real person of Jesus, the same Jesus that was responded to by the four Gospel writers, and who has been known in the church throughout the ages.

The revelation of God in Christ

If you ask what idea of revelation this suggests, it will not be that revelation consists in a set of true sentences dictated by God. What we have is the impact of the person and teachings of Jesus on those who heard them, on those who transmitted them over decades, on those who translated them into Greek, on those who edited them into four very different Gospels, and on those who have helped us to understand the Gospels in specific ways by their commentaries and interpretations. We are not talking about inerrant sentences here. We are talking about the recorded revelatory impact of a charismatic personality, which brought people to see their lives in relation to God in a new way. And we are talking about reflection on this impact over many centuries in many diverse cultures and in many different circumstances.

Jesus' person gave others great insights into the nature and purpose of God, and the divine will for human life. Jesus must have had such insight himself, but he was no philosopher. He was a man of prayer, devoted to God, with a mission to proclaim that God was drawing near in a new way, to proclaim the kingdom of God. His personal relation to God was definitive of his life. Jesus lived in union with ultimate reality. His disciples felt that he was one with God in a unique way, making him fit to be the ruler in God's kingdom, the one who shows what God is truly like.

So the revelation in Jesus is a matter of his personal apprehension of the divine, which transformed his human life by its power and love. It is not a matter of Jesus' reception of inerrant sentences detailing the nature of the Trinity. It is a matter of his direct experience of God, his extraordinary wisdom and healing power, and his unique historical placing as the fulfilment of messianic expectation within the Judaism of his day.

The apostles felt the impact of Jesus' life, and no doubt remembered, handed on orally, and recorded many of his sayings and the main events of his life. In particular, they themselves experienced his resurrection in a series of extraordinary appearances to them, and that experience illumined in retrospect all they remembered of his life.

Then these oral traditions were passed down in various churches, in which further experiences of the risen Christ, though now not in bodily form, occurred, and in which the Spirit of Christ was experienced, transforming lives for the better and increasing the ability of men and women to love the poor and outcast, in an astounding way. These traditions were collected into "Gospels", testimonies related in edited oral memories of Jesus' acts and teachings.

Finally, four Gospels and a number of letters from church leaders to their young congregations were embodied in a sacred canon, which became a sort of touchstone of authenticity for the continuing experiences of the risen Christ in churches which became increasingly diverse. The church interpreted these writings in a specific way – or in a number of specific ways as the years went by – and built up a picture of the role of Jesus in God's purpose for the world. This picture came to be outlined in the great Greek creeds of the early centuries – and basic concepts of Greek philosophy were used to do so.

At each stage of this process, experience is of paramount importance – not just personal and subjective experiences, but also experiences of objective events, of visions, and of communal testimonies to a divine transforming and healing power. Reflective interpretation is secondary, yet it is essential to the process of seeing the nature of the God revealed in Jesus.

Given this process, what is the character of Christian revelation? Jesus did not, like Muhammad, claim to recite the words of God, which were to be faithfully recorded in the original language. Jesus was claimed – and, I think, claimed himself – to be the disclosure of the character of God in human form and the one whose resurrection assured people of the will of God to redeem estranged humanity. But we do not have inerrant and completely consistent records of Jesus' life. We do not have the actual words of God. What we have are varied interpretations of four diverse edited remembered traditions deriving from oral records of how the apostles experienced Jesus. These records presuppose that Jesus had a uniquely intimate and intense experience of God, a completeness of empowerment by God, and a unique role in the prophetic history of Israel, that make it appropriate to see him as the human act and image of the invisible God.

Is that enough for faith? It does not enable us to say that everything said about Jesus in the Gospels is true. Too much later interpretation and too many later experiences are incorporated into the accounts we have for that. We might expect that some passages in the Gospels will have been misremembered, or have been edited to suit the editor's vision of Christian faith, or will remain almost wholly puzzling. But we might also expect that an accurate general picture of Jesus will have been retained, and that many of the more memorable sayings will give an authentic flavour of his teaching.

We can therefore regard the New Testament writings as "inspired" by God, in the sense that, as the second Vatican Council of the Roman Catholic Church put it in 1965, "The books of Scripture firmly, faithfully and without error, teach that truth which God, for the sake of our salvation, wished to see confided to the sacred Scriptures."[3] What is wholly reliable (even inerrant) in Scripture are those truths which are important for our salvation – truths about Jesus' death and resurrection and about the kingdom of God – but not the exact words Jesus used in his teaching ministry. That is enough to enable someone to say that "in Christ God was reconciling the world to himself" (2 Corinthians 5:19) and that through Christ God can still be encountered in life-changing ways. Indeed, as I shall argue, it is very important that the person of Jesus should evoke different personal responses in different people and in different cultures, so that revelation should remain dynamic and life-changing, not fossilized in the exact words of a long-dead culture.

Part 2
Universal Salvation: The True Gospel
Parables of the Community of the Disciples of Christ

The kingdom of God

There are many things we do not know about Jesus of Nazareth, but one thing that seems pretty certain is that he went about Galilee and Judaea teaching that people should repent, because "the kingdom of heaven has come near" (Matthew 3:2; Matthew uses "heaven" as a circumlocution for "God"). Strange as it may seem, there has never been complete agreement among Christians about what exactly he meant by this. Some, including eminent scholars like Albert Schweitzer, thought that he expected a sudden interruption of the course of history by a miraculous act of God. The Day of Judgment – a day of terror and wrath – would come soon, within a generation. Then God would inaugurate a new age of peace and holiness, when scattered Jewish tribes would return to Jerusalem, and all nations would come to the Jerusalem Temple to worship God. A major problem with this view is that it never happened, and so Jesus has to be seen as a deluded millenarian prophet – not a good start for a great spiritual teacher!

Schweitzer and Johannes Weiss, in their attempt to develop what is usually known in English as a "thoroughgoing eschatology", were partly reacting against German liberal theologians like Harnack, who thought that Jesus regarded the kingdom of heaven solely as the inner rule of the Spirit of God in the hearts of men and women. For on that liberal view, what happens to traditional beliefs in the reign of Christ in heaven and the return of Christ in glory, and to talk of judgment and resurrection as real future occurrences?

That is the question I propose to address. My answer will be nearer the liberal view than to Schweitzer, but it will give more weight to the objective reality and hope of the "return of Christ" and to the afterlife, judgment, and general resurrection of the dead as factual expectations.

My starting point is that Schweitzer's type of account does not make it reasonable to worship Christ, or to see Christ as the fulfilment of human history, or as the saviour of the world. It does not make it reasonable to see Jesus as a profound spiritual teacher at all. So, in what a historian might regard as a thought-experiment, I want to make the assumption that Jesus was a profound spiritual teacher, and see how we might then interpret the Gospel records of his teachings.

The longest attempt in the Synoptic Gospels to present Jesus' teachings is to be found in the "Sermon on the Mount", in Matthew's Gospel, chapters 5–7. I consider this to be a profound statement of a spiritual teaching that on the whole could only have come from a uniquely insightful prophet, and that has the power to challenge and transform the hearts and minds of those who read it in every age and time.

The scholarly consensus of most biblical scholars is that the sermon is a collection of sayings edited by the Gospel writer, sayings which had been passed down in oral traditions for some years. Moreover they are in a language, Greek, which was probably not used by Jesus in his teaching. So they are not the actual words of Jesus, and almost certainly not written in the order in which he said them, in one continuous oration. Nevertheless, they carry a distinctive imprint and style which marks them as the products of a supreme spiritual intelligence. In that sense, I believe that they are on the whole, and despite some secondary interpretation, authentic records of the teaching of Jesus. I believe the statements in the Sermon form a prime textual basis for Christian belief in God as a God of self-giving love. In that sense, they are so distinctive and important that they form a standard against which all other reported sayings of Jesus, and indeed all the spiritual teachings of the Bible – in both Old and New Testaments – may be assessed. In my opinion they go to the heart of Jesus' teaching, and so they help to form a view of what Jesus meant by the kingdom of heaven.

The Sermon is notoriously difficult to interpret. Interpretations have varied enormously. Albert Schweitzer saw in it an "interim ethic" much of which is totally irrelevant to us, because it was meant for people who had only a short time to live before the end of the world. Catholic tradition has distinguished between "counsels of perfection" and "precepts of morality", the former being for monks, nuns, and saints who pursue perfection, while the latter are for more ordinary mortals. Radical Reformers have seen it as a call for marginal groups within society (for instance, Quakers or Mennonites) to act as a challenge and catalyst within the wider society. Luther distinguished between what is binding in public life and the stricter rules that apply only in personal life, while later Lutherans thought the Sermon placed before humans an "impossible possibility", that it was both binding and impossible to fulfil (and therefore forced humans to rely solely on grace).

My own view, elaborated in *The Rule of Love*, is that the Sermon places before all Christians a set of attitudes or virtues which are ideals that the Spirit gradually shapes in us. These are not just unrealizable ideals, though the extent to which they can be realized will vary in differing situations. Their existence will always make a significant difference to the way Christians act. This view may be largely aligned with Stanley Hauerwas's powerful presentation of Christian ethics,[1] and with its philosophical background in Alasdair MacIntyre's work. It will become clear, however, that my feeling for the tragic compromises of historical life also owes much to Reinhold Niebuhr and leads me to distance myself from the radical pacifist stance that Hauerwas and John Yoder commend. I will give reasons for this interpretation in Part 4 of this book, but for now I will use it to help to give my general interpretation of Jesus' ethical teaching, and I hope the view would be broadly acceptable to Christians, even if their specific interpretation of the Sermon differs from mine.

The interpretation we give clearly depends on a more general background view of Jesus' person and mission. This background view will probably be derived from some form of life within a Christian community, which we may have modified in the light of our own personal experience. The reading of the Sermon will itself be one source of such modifications. My background supposition is that Jesus offered eternal life to all who turn to him, that he died to unite humankind to God, and that he rose to reign in glory. This leads me to look for a profound spiritual teaching which teaches important truths about the relation of humanity to God in the Sermon, rather than, for instance, a set of interim rules based on predictions (which turned out to be false) about what would happen in Jerusalem in the very near future. If the Sermon can be plausibly interpreted in such a way, then that interpretation will in turn cast light on the interpretation of the other recorded teachings of Jesus in the Gospels.

I will begin by offering a personal interpretation of the Beatitudes (Matthew 5:3–12), which form a prelude to the Sermon, and then of the Sermon itself. The italicized sections in this book, almost all from the Sermon on the Mount and from the parables, mark where I have provided my own interpretation of the biblical texts. I would issue a reminder that I am not claiming to give the one correct meaning of the text. My intention is to show how the text can be read as a profound spiritual document, not just a collection of rather cryptic moral pronouncements.

I thereby intend to suggest that original biblical texts are most properly used as the basis for such personal interpretations. The Sermon is a spiritual text that is meant to evoke a personal sense of the nature and purpose of God, and whose meaning cannot be exhausted by any one account. If my interpretation is within the range of intelligible readings, it will serve as an introduction to a fuller interpretation of the teaching of Jesus as a set of richly metaphorical or symbolic texts with many possible connotations, but with a core of central metaphors and symbols that point to a positive gospel of the unlimitedly forgiving and liberating love of God.

I will speak of "spiritual metaphors", meaning that things or properties may be described in physical terms that are not literally true (for instance, Jesus is described as king of the Jews, and Paradise is described as "Abraham's bosom", even though Jesus is not literally the king of Judah, and the redeemed do not sit on Abraham's chest). Such statements are not literally true, but they have the function of suggesting spiritual truths. Jesus is the spiritual king in the kingdom of God, and the redeemed will be with Abraham in the world to come.

Such statements are false in their normal or primary usage, but suggest a deep spiritual truth, though it is not spelled out in detail, and may suggest slightly different things to different people. My aim is to show that the majority of the sayings ascribed to Jesus in the Gospels are most adequately taken as being or as containing spiritual metaphors.

In the light of this, I think that Schweitzer's approach will be seen to be too literalistic and too negative in its stress on the wrath and judgment and rigorous exclusivity of God and of the gospel of Jesus. Eschatology may be present in Jesus' teaching, but it is not nearly as literal as Schweitzer and Weiss thought.

This, then, is an interpretation of the Beatitudes that does not simply take them literally or at face value, but that seeks for a deeper spiritual meaning, achieved by thinking of "the poor", "those who mourn", and "the hungry" as apparently physical descriptions which are in fact spiritual metaphors. The meek, the merciful, the pure in heart, the peacemakers, and the persecuted seem to be straightforward descriptions, but they too are taken in a wider sense than the plain descriptions might suggest, so as to refer broadly to inner attitudes of mind or spirit.

The way to the kingdom of heaven (the rule of God in the lives of men and women):

Those who enter the kingdom of heaven do not seek to possess the things of this world. They are non-attached and do not grieve the loss of what must pass away and cease to be.

Those who enter the kingdom of heaven are kind and compassionate, seeking to comfort those who mourn and to rejoice with those who have good fortune.

Those who enter the kingdom of heaven do not think of themselves as superior to others, or insist upon deference to their position and achievements.

Those who enter the kingdom of heaven seek justice for the oppressed and the welfare of all without exception.

Those who enter the kingdom of heaven show mercy to those who are weak, and forgive those who seek to turn from evil.

Those who enter the kingdom of heaven love what is beautiful and good, and turn away from all that expresses hatred and violence.

Those who enter the kingdom of heaven pursue all that fulfils human life and builds up friendship and love.

Those who enter the kingdom of heaven will endure hardship and enmity in order to witness to the supremacy of loving-kindness and selfless love.

A more literal interpretation of these Beatitudes is possible, especially as given in the original Greek, and in its Lucan version (Luke 6:20–26). The poor, the hungry, and those who weep will laugh and be filled, says Luke's version, while the rich, the replete, and those who laugh and are respected will weep and be hungry.

There are two problems with such a literal interpretation. First, it seems to lack spiritual depth. It just predicts a reversal of fortunes, regardless of the character of the people concerned, and expresses a vengeful resentment of the rich and powerful. These are spiritual vices, not virtues. Second, the prediction is false; it never happened. That may not in itself shake a person's faith in the spiritual pre-eminence of Jesus, but there are textual reasons to think that these teachings were taken in a spiritual sense very early on. There is no overwhelming reason to suppose that Jesus himself did not do so.

Matthew begins to do so by adding the phrases "poor in spirit" and "hunger and thirst for righteousness" to his account. This need to interpret texts spiritually is clear also in Luke's account of Jesus' first (and possibly last!) sermon at Nazareth (Luke 4:16–21). Jesus here says: "the Spirit... has anointed me to bring good news to the poor... release to the captives, and recovery of sight to the blind, to let the oppressed go free... Today this Scripture has been fulfilled in your hearing." But as Jesus spoke in the synagogue at Nazareth, no prisoners were literally released, no slaves were literally set free. He brought good news to those who had need of God, who were prisoners of greed and hatred, who were blind to the presence of God, and who were slaves of disordered passion.

What was the good news? That they would, in a very near earthly future, see and know God, and be freed from oppression in a wholly just and compassionate society? Some have interpreted it thus. But this too was literally false. All those to whom he spoke died in an unjust, repressive society under the military dictatorship of Rome.

When Luke gives Mary a song in the house of Zechariah, she sings, "He has scattered the proud... he has brought down the powerful from their thrones and lifted up the lowly; he has filled the hungry with good things, and sent the rich away empty" (Luke 1:51–53). But that never literally happened. The powerful still sit on their thrones or presidential seats, and millions still die of hunger every year.

Luke also gives Zechariah a song at the presentation of Jesus in the Temple (Luke 1:68–79), writing that God has acted so that "we being rescued from the hands of our enemies, might serve him without fear". But Israel was not delivered from Rome. In a few years Rome totally destroyed Israel and wiped it from the map.

If these statements were true (and I believe that they were), they were not literally true. Just as "the poor" has a spiritual meaning: "those who lack, but wish for, God" (however much money they have), so "the feast" that fills the hungry has a spiritual meaning: "seeing and knowing God" (however much food they have or do not have).

If this is correct, the kingdom cannot be seen as a future earthly kingdom. It is primarily an inward and spiritual kingdom, the rule of the Spirit in the heart. That is what Jesus brings near by his presence. If this is so, it affirms something of crucial importance for the interpretation of Jesus' teachings. They will be metaphorical or symbolic, not literal. And they will refer primarily to inner spiritual realities, though they will also refer to future spiritual realities that are not just the states of individual human minds. Spiritual reality is real and objective, and it is what is referred to by the great metaphors of Jesus' teaching. It is therefore vital to uncover the meaning of these metaphors, even though it is part of metaphorical speech that it will suggest a number of related meanings, none of which is the only and fully adequate correct one.

What follows is a personal reading of the Sermon, which seeks to find in it a picture of the sort of person whose life is filled with the Spirit of God. If such a reading is plausible that may suggest this as at least one important strand of its meaning, which gives it direct relevance to Christian lives in every age. It will specify the ideal values that should mark the life of a disciple of Jesus.

The commandments of the heart

Those who keep the law of God will not kill; nor will they give way to anger or contempt. They will seek to heal and meet conflict with patience and understanding, so far as is possible.

They will not commit adultery; nor will they destroy faithful friendships; nor will they allow selfish passion to destroy loyalty and faithfulness.

• *They will not lie; nor will they deceive, mislead, or fail to seek the truth, whether it is pleasing or not.*

They will not take vengeance; nor will they knowingly cause harm even to those who do evil, except with the intention of bringing them to good.

They will not hate anyone, even their enemies; nor will they allow personal feelings to prevent them from aiming at the welfare of all sentient beings.

They will not do good or parade their piety ostentatiously, in order to be esteemed by others, but they will act always and secretly for the sake of good alone.

They will be merciful and forgiving, not remembering old offences but being always ready to start relationships anew.

They will not pursue wealth and possessions for themselves, but will use what they have for the well-being of others.

They will not be anxious about the future, or regretful about the past; but they will be prudent and look with hope to the future, seeking the way of heaven above all things.

They will not be judgmental or vindictive towards others, but will be self-aware, and mindful of the possibilities for good that lie within themselves.

They will treat others as they would wish others to treat them.

They will love that which is good for its own sake, and they will love others as they love themselves.

To "look for the kingdom of heaven" is to seek this way (taken from Matthew 5:17 – 7:29, while the final sentence is taken from Matthew 22:34–40, because I really think it fits well into the Sermon!) above all things. It is to seek a life that is liberated from egoism, greed, pride, hatred, and anxiety. It is to seek a life that is filled with loving-kindness, moderation, joy in the welfare of others, universal compassion, and equanimity.

Taking such an interpretation, what Jesus was saying was something like, "This life – the kingdom life – has come near" (Matthew 4:17). The Greek word translated as "come near" is *ēngiken*. The verb is in the perfect tense, and so it refers to a completed action whose consequences are still present. It does not say that the kingdom has arrived in its fullness, so there remains a future element, of something yet to be completed. But something has definitely happened, and it has brought the kingdom near. It is not far away or beyond your reach. It is a possibility for you. It is within your reach.

How can we enter into such a life? By a turning of the mind away from self and concern with self, and by letting that life – which is other and higher than ours, yet comes to us from within – suffuse our own. This is a turning from individual mind – from my ego-driven self – to universal spirit – to the inner self of all things – which comes near to us as we hear the one who speaks the words of life. To enter the kingdom of heaven is to live the Spirit-filled life. That, in my view, is the first and most essential, though not the only, meaning of the symbol of the kingdom.

Parables

I will now extend this analysis to the more general teachings of Jesus, as they are recorded in the Synoptic Gospels, in order to bring out the way in which I think Jesus' teaching can be received and understood by contemporary disciples. Interpreted thus, the teachings do not show Jesus to be a deluded apocalyptic prophet of the end of the world. They reveal him to be a teacher who gives insight into the deepest spiritual realities of human life in relation to God and God's purpose for the world.

I shall concentrate on the parables, as narratives that are most characteristic of the teaching method Jesus used. I am, of course, aware that there have been many profound treatments of Jesus' parables, and I am not attempting to replace them or improve them. I believe close linguistic analyses and research into the social context of the parables to be a necessary foundation of any plausible interpretation. As a philosopher and doctrinal theologian my main competence is in the conceptual analysis of religious language, and in the historical development of Christian doctrines. For knowledge of the linguistic and cultural background of Jesus' teachings, and for close analysis of the biblical documents, I need to rely on the arguments and conclusions of New Testament scholars. As a Christian, I start from the general position outlined in the first part of this book. I need to know whether New Testament research supports such a view, whether it calls for qualifications and modifications of the view, or whether perhaps it simply allows the view as one possibility among others.

There is no doubt that the parables are central to the teaching of the kingdom. Since I want to relate my view to what it is reasonable to think the views of Jesus himself were, I shall be presupposing the hard work that New Testament scholars have done. But my aim is to defend, as well as I can, a particular view of the Christian gospel for today, which is rooted in the New Testament documents themselves.

In Matthew's Gospel the parables are said to be "mysteries" (Matthew 13:11), and I think we should take this with full seriousness. They are not obvious, clear, and straightforward. Even when the Gospels record an explanation given to the disciples, any apparent clarity is misleading. Indeed the explanations often seem to diffuse the whole point of the parable, by making it too much like an allegory, where each element of the parable points to some symbolized reality, and you can gain a word for word translation into literal discourse. Although such an approach was widespread before the nineteenth century, since Adolf Jülicher's work (*Die Gleichnisreden Jesu*) it has been generally repudiated.

C.H. Dodd thought that the statement that the parables are mysteries is unlikely to be original with Jesus, and that it, along with the allegorical explanations of a few parables, are rather weak commentaries by early Christians.[2] I agree that the allegories given are fairly unconvincing. Indeed they seem to make all mystery disappear into something that is all too clear. But I think there is a real point in saying that the parables conceal something, and something important.

A mystery is something, as all the Synoptic Gospels assert, the point of which can be misunderstood by those whose ears are not ready to hear it, but whose meaning is given to those who are open to the message of the kingdom. It therefore misses the point to try to give a strictly allegorical interpretation. For a mystery must remain allusive, cryptic, and hidden. It must be given personally to each one who is ready to be initiated into the mystery. And the mystery is not a mere intellectual or verbal understanding. It is a participation in a hidden divine reality, a living in the eternal word of God which can never be adequately spoken in human sentences. As I hope will gradually become apparent, the fundamental mystery of the parables is concealed, not in the words themselves, but in the person who speaks them. A parable, as spoken by Jesus, is meant to evoke a transforming insight and a uniquely personal apprehension of God. It is an insight into the nature of Jesus and an apprehension of divine presence in him. That insight and apprehension is the mystery hidden from those who hear only a story or an allegory.

As well as the essentially mysterious and non-verbal function of parables, it is important to see the parable teaching of Jesus as a whole. Individual parables, taken out of context, may, as I shall show, be very misleading. The whole body of parables provides a dialectical and holistic pattern of meaning, in which contrary themes balance one another, and the whole is greater than the sum of the parts.

Of course the Gospels give only a selection of Jesus' parables, and so we do not possess them as a whole, as given by Jesus. It is not even always clear which stories in the New Testament should be called parables, in this sense. I have not tried to make any sort of definitive, or even approximate, list. So I have included some stories which may indeed be more like allegories, and I may have omitted some which have that character of hidden spiritual truth that parables should have. Nevertheless we can see that there are groups of parables with different emphases, and it is important to balance these emphases to gain an insight into Jesus' teaching. I shall show that a failure to seek such a holistic balance can lead to some uncharitable and judgmental interpretations of Jesus' teaching, and I shall try to justify the balance that I find in the Gospels.

In case this sounds too obscure even for parables, I shall give one example of what I mean. Some parables seem to be very judgmental and exclusive (speaking of burning fruitless trees or tares on a rubbish heap, or excluding people from the wedding feast). It is important to balance these parables with other parables that speak of divine forgiveness and which include even sinners and enemies in the scope of the divine love (obviously, the parables of the lost sheep and the good Samaritan come into this group). If we get the balance of these parables wrong, the consequences will not be helpful. So I shall do my best to justify the sort of balance that I think is appropriate. And, as I have suggested, one major clue to help in this task is the teaching of the Sermon on the Mount, which I think provides a fairly clear indication of the direction which interpretations of Jesus' teachings should take.

Joachim Jeremias, in his major work on the parables, aimed to get to the original meaning of the parables, behind the accretions made by the early church to the earliest attainable form of Jesus' parabolic teaching. Other scholars are sceptical about whether this can really be done, but for most people Jeremias established pretty well that the church has both preserved the central elements of Jesus' teaching, and has added interpretative material of its own.

I am not primarily concerned, however, with the detailed meaning of specific parables, or with Jeremias's argument that they are rooted in very specific topical occasions of utterance in Jesus' life. I want to know if there is a spiritual teaching about how to be liberated from sin and brought into union with God to be found in the parables. For this purpose I have divided the parables into three main groups: parables about the liberated life, about the community through which this life is proclaimed (the church, in her many forms), and about the final goal of union with God (partly framed in the apocalyptic imagery of the "end of the age").

In my brief italicized summaries of the parables, I have indicated my own personal interpretation of them and have sometimes run together passages from different parts of the Gospels that seem to exhibit thematic similarities. Purists may complain that this treatment blurs important nuances of the Greek text and runs together things which should be kept separate. My defence is that such important textual work has been ably done by others. My aim is to present a set of personal interpretations which build up into a general theological response to the parables, and to see whether these interpretations form a consistent, coherent, and plausible whole. If they do, they may suggest one perspective from which to see the teaching of Jesus, and that will in turn be the foundation for a theology of the Gospels which can claim to be a faithful response to the text, without claiming to elicit its one definitive and unique meaning.

I shall begin with a set of parables which I take to be at least in part about the community of the new covenant, the covenant written in the heart, about which the prophet Jeremiah writes (Jeremiah 31:31–34), and of which Jesus is taken by the New Testament writers to be the fulfilment. Among these I would place the parable of the sower, one of the best known parables, and one which speaks of how the preaching of the kingdom is differently received by different hearers. I must acknowledge that this is precisely one of the parables that C.H. Dodd regards as being saddled with a misleading allegorical interpretation. The parable, he thinks, originally just said that good results can be produced by hard work, even though with difficulty. But I have to say that in this case I find the little allegory quite helpful. I think that the mention of birds, rocks, sun, and thorns is just too detailed and precise to be without significant meaning. The only problem is that the meaning is so obvious that the disciples must have been particularly stupid not to see it. So I think that the "explanation" of the parable given in the Gospels leaves the "mystery" intact and unexpressed – the mystery of the central role of Jesus in both sowing and reaping the harvest, and the mystery of the church as the community of those in whom the seeds of the kingdom grow.

The sower

Some hear that the kingdom of heaven has come near, but they are preoccupied with the pursuit of wealth, power, or fame, and they pay no heed.

Some hear of the kingdom of heaven, and embrace it eagerly. But times of difficulty and hardship come, and they lose courage and resolve, and they do not persist.

Some hear of the kingdom of heaven, but the riches and pleasures of the world prove too strong, and they fall away.

Some hear of the kingdom of heaven, and it takes root in them, and they grow in love, in joy, peace, and patience, in kindness, generosity, and faithfulness, in gentleness and self-control. That is where the kingdom of heaven is. (from Matthew 13:1–9)

In this parable, the kingdom is something that can take root in human lives and that produces a fruitful yield. I have added Galatians 5:22 to my personal reading of the parable. This addition may seem odd from a strictly scholarly point of view, since biblical scholars tend to think that we should not overlook important differences of context in different parts of Scripture. They are right, of course. But I am seeking readings that convey spiritual insight, and sometimes putting together similar metaphors from different parts of Scripture – of grain or fruit in this case – can do that, as long as we do not forget the differences. I am not suggesting that the biblical writers or editors made such a connection. I am suggesting that this sort of connection can be made in a spiritual reading, as long as we do not fall into the trap of asserting that it is the "one true" connection, and as long as we realize that we are indulging in a personal imaginative play of images to try to provide new insights into how to live as a disciple of Jesus.

With that strong proviso, we might say that, with regard to the "fruits" of the kingdom:

• Love comes first, as the most basic attitude of the Spirit-led life, a selfless concern for the well-being of all others, without exception.

• Joy is next, as a characteristic of the life of faith, which is continuously refreshed by the knowledge of the presence and love of God.

• Peace or equanimity and calmness of mind is a quality of a mind not distracted by the everyday troubles of the world, but self-possessed and mindful.

• Patience is needed to guard against the tendency to force things to go as one wishes. We must act without fretting that results do not seem to come quickly enough, and we must leave the outcome of our actions to God in hope.

• Kindness is a simple virtue, too often overlooked, which never regards others with contempt or indifference, but which seeks to make them feel valued for what they are and can yet be.

- Generosity is the disposition to do more than is required of one, to think the best of others, and to share the good things we have.

- Faithfulness entails keeping one's promises, being concerned to preserve and build up friendships, and being trustworthy and honest in all one's dealings.

- Gentleness treats others tenderly, not seeking either to dominate or to be blindly subservient, but to encourage the realization of human capacities for creativity and goodness.

- Self-control is not blinded by passion or carried away by anger, greed, or hatred. Its aim is sure and its pursuit is calm, shaping all things to the attainment of the goal, which is conscious union with the supreme Good.

If we live by the Spirit, this is what we shall become as we grow into the fullness of the kingdom.

The phrase "kingdom of God" is not common in Paul, but in the parable of the sower, at least in Matthew's Gospel, membership of the kingdom seems to be a quality of life, a quality that is produced by the Spirit of God. In the Synoptic Gospels, John the Baptist is recorded as saying that Jesus will "baptize with the Holy Spirit and with fire" (Matthew 3:11). So when the kingdom takes root, it is the Spirit who produces the fruits of character and compassionate action that characterize the kingdom life.

The parable also reminds us that, attractive though it may be, the way is difficult, and few are able to walk in it. Its beauty attracts us; but its rigour condemns us. If we are tempted to think that we are among the righteous, this parable leaves us in no doubt that we are probably not. We live in darkness, far from the kingdom of heaven. Yet in proclaiming that the kingdom has come near, Jesus teaches that, while we cannot attain the kingdom life, it draws near to us. That is his good news, not that there is a good time coming soon for those who have no money (the literal interpretation of the coming of the kingdom in Luke 1:53), but that those who strive for goodness, but realize their spiritual weakness, will be forgiven, reconciled, and renewed by the gift and power of the Spirit.

The mustard seed and the yeast of the world
God's kingdom will grow throughout the earth, until it exerts an influence over all human life.

A mustard seed is tiny, but it grows to produce a large bush (Matthew 13:31). When yeast is mixed with flour, it permeates the whole mixture, and makes bread rise (Matthew 13:33). Seeds sown in the ground grow of their own accord, and when the crop is ready, it is harvested (Mark 4:26).

These short parables depict the kingdom as something that will grow from small beginnings, until it permeates the whole world. It produces a crop that, when it is fully mature, will be gathered to God. C.H. Dodd denies that these parables are speaking of a long period during which the church might grow throughout the world,[3] until a final harvest comes. He agrees that the early church, and the Gospel editor, probably thought that. But Jesus, he supposes, was thinking of the harvest as taking place in his lifetime, even as he spoke, and the growth as having come to completion with his own proclamation that the kingdom had come, and was already present in the world. The harvest is now taking place as Jesus and the disciples proclaim the kingdom, and, Dodd says, "It does not seem necessary to suppose that the judgment is treated as a new event in the future."[4]

This fascinating suggestion is rejected by those who accept Albert Schweitzer's view of Jesus as an apocalyptic millenarian, but it coheres well with Jesus' statement at Matthew 9:37–38: "The harvest is plentiful, but the labourers are few. Therefore ask the Lord of the harvest to send out labourers into his harvest." The problem with it is that it seems to cut out any reference to the future, any thought of the gospel as something to be preached throughout the whole world, and any belief in a final judgment that transcends the present moment. It is true that Jesus is portrayed in the Gospels as having a ministry only to the Jewish people. But it is hard to think that a great spiritual teacher would have no conception of the whole Gentile world as an object of God's redemptive love. And if Jesus did think of himself as instrumental in bringing into being a community of the new covenant, it seems likely that he would have had some idea that this community might fulfil the vocation of the ancient covenant community, to bring knowledge of the presence of God to the whole world.

I therefore think that Dodd is right to stress that Jesus is not *just* talking about some future event, whether near or far away in time. He is right to portray the kingdom as breaking into the world in a new way in the ministry of Jesus. But there is no need to deny that Jesus' ministry will carry on after his death in a new way, and that the kingdom will continue to grow until it enlivens the whole world. And there is no need to confine the judgment to what happens at the time of Jesus.

Dodd speaks powerfully of a conviction "central to the Christian faith, that at a particular point in time and space, the eternal entered decisively into history".[5] The phrase is central to the thought of Friedrich Schleiermacher, who spoke of true religion as "the sense and taste of the infinite", and it is, I think, central to Christian spirituality to see all things temporal and finite in the light of eternity and infinity. Jesus himself is spoken of as "the image of the invisible God" (Colossians 1:15); in him the eternal God becomes present in time and space. Yet it is important to see that the eternal is more and other than the temporal, and that its entrance into time is not confined to the life of Jesus.

In other places, Dodd speaks of "the impact upon this world of the powers of the world to come".[6] He says, "When he [Jesus] spoke of it [the kingdom] in terms of the future his words suggest, not any readjustment of conditions on this earth, but the glories of a world beyond this."[7] There is "a world beyond this", a "world to come", with its own activity and powers. Thus not only does eternity enter into time: equally importantly, every human moment of time is taken into eternity, into a more glorious world beyond this. That is something future, something yet to come, even though it will not be on this physical earth.

I think, therefore, that there is a future reference when the parables speak of a "harvest" of growing corn. But the reference is to a future beyond the time of this world. It does not matter whether this worldly time will end soon, or after a few thousand years, or after billions of years of cosmic history. What matters is that the kingdom spreads throughout the world of time, opening the way to a world beyond our time, where all that has been done in time is brought to completion. That is not quite what Dodd meant by "realized eschatology", but it is more like what Joachim Jeremias spoke of as "an eschatology that is in process of realization",[8] and Dodd agreed with this expression in correspondence.[9] There will in the future be a fulfilment of all things, but that future is not on this earth, whether near or far away. In this world, the kingdom will grow until it covers the earth, and perhaps even all inhabited worlds.

This mustard bush, this yeast, and these seeds, will bring blessing to the whole world. So the kingdom begins in a small insignificant province of the Roman Empire. But it grows until it enlightens the world. Then the kingdom of the Spirit will no longer be confined to Jews (though Jews will not finally be rejected, as Romans 11 makes clear). It will be opened to all who accept Christ as king, and accept their vocation as his ambassadors to bring the justice and mercy of God near, by letting God rule in and through them.

When Jesus proclaimed that the kingdom had drawn near, I do not believe that he could have thought it was only open to Jews, or to a few people around the eastern Mediterranean. For the kingdom is not the company of those who are secure in their own salvation, while the rest of the world remains lost in darkness. It is the company of those who seek to heal the world and make it whole, to be "branches upon which many birds can find rest" and "leaven which enlivens the whole world", to bring "the powers of the world to come" into each present time.

The pearl

God's kingdom is like a pearl which is worth more than everything you possess, or like treasure hidden in a field.

The kingdom that grows like mustard seed or yeast throughout the earth can plausibly be seen as the church, the community of the disciples of Christ, in all her varied forms and manifestations. We must be continually critical of its tendencies to corruption and power, while being supportive of its works of wisdom, beauty, and love.

The kingdom that is worth giving up everything for (Matthew 13:44–46) is the kingdom within the heart, which seeks for the clear vision of God, and empowerment by selfless love. It anticipates the ultimate aim and goal of creation, the kingdom of the new creation, where all things temporal fade into insignificance before the vision of eternal beauty. It is worth renouncing everything ("the world") to follow the way that leads to its attainment.

Yet the world is not simply negated by the kingdom. Spiritual beauty is naturally and properly expressed in material forms, and we come to know it through knowing its finite forms. It is only after the world of time has run its course, at the "end of all things", that all the beauties of the world can be finally taken up into the beauty of eternity. In this way, eternity progressively expresses and unfolds itself in time. But the things of time find their true expression and fulfilment only when they are taken into the life of eternity. The kingdom comes near to us and expresses itself in us; and we are taken into the kingdom and find our fulfilment in God. That is the mystery of the pearl without price. For now it is buried or hidden in the recesses of the individual self. But its presence within us is the anticipation of the final unity of all things in the universal Self.

The lost sheep

If a shepherd loses a sheep, he will look for it, and if he finds it, he will rejoice greatly. Or if a poor woman loses a coin, she will do everything she can to find it, and if she does, she will rejoice. So God does not want to lose anyone, but calls on sinners to repent.

These short parables (Luke 15:3 and 15:8) revolve around the theme of God's seeking out those who are lost in the cares and desires of the world, and God's joy when they find their true selves in God. God is not unmoved and unchanging. God acts to do as much as possible, without infringing the freedom of creatures, to seek them out and offer forgiveness when they have turned away. The life of men and women who pursue wealth, power, or possessions for their own sakes misses the mark of true humanity (that is what "sin" – *hamartia* – means). Such things give no lasting joy. The value of a thing does not lie in that it gives me what I want, but in its inherent worth, which I can never possess but may contemplate with gratitude.

In the life of Jesus, God shows what is of true inherent value – a life of compassion, healing, forgiveness, kindness, and self-denial for the sake of goodness. If we live such a life, we will be rooted in God's love for us and for the created world, and that love will fill us with a joy that none can take away. God seeks and God rejoices. God shares in human sufferings, but God is not defeated by suffering. After the cross comes resurrection. God raises human lives to eternal joy. So the marks of the Christian life are practical concern for those who are in need or in despair, and joy in the knowledge of the presence of God, who, though God might change in the ways in which the divine love is expressed, will never change in passionate care that all created souls will find a fulfilment of their unique personal potentialities, and joy in their conscious unity with the divine life.

That balanced combination of imperishable joy and self-denial can perhaps only be fully found in our human world in Jesus, the one who feasted with publicans and sinners, yet also accepted the cross as the ultimate price of his loyalty to the divine will. But it is the human ideal for which each of us should strive. And it is a profound Christian insight into the character of God, who enters into the suffering of the fallen world in order to bring human lives to eternal joy.

The feast

The kingdom of heaven is like a great feast. The patriarchs of Israel are there, Abraham, Isaac, and Jacob. The people of Israel, especially the religious leaders, are invited. But many decline the invitation and do not come. So many others are invited, from every point of the compass, especially the poor, the blind, and the lame, both good and bad. Nevertheless, those who refuse to clothe themselves with penitence and justice will be excluded from the feast.

This passage (Luke 14:15–24 and Matthew 22:1–14, adding the partly analogous story in Matthew 8:11–12) relates the kingdom specifically to the history of Israel. The patriarchs were not, in fact, men of perfected morality. Jacob, in particular, was a spectacular deceiver, and Abraham was a pretty shifty character, quite capable even of denying that he was married when it seemed politic to do so (Genesis 12:20). Yet they share in the feast. Their penitence and trust in God is accepted by God ("Abraham believed God, and it was reckoned to him as righteousness", Romans 4:3). The kingdom is here specifically connected to observance of the *Torah* (the laws of Moses, found in written form in the first five books of the Bible, and in oral form in the Talmud) and to the covenant between God and the descendants of Abraham.

The person of Jesus cannot be taken out of its historical context. God made a covenant with Abraham and his descendants that they would serve God, and God would be known to them in a special way. God's choice comes first, not human excellence or attainment. For Jesus, that covenant remains in force. Indeed, through his life and teaching it receives a renewed and more internal realization:

> I will make a new covenant with the house of Israel...
> says the Lord... I will put my law within them, and I will
> write it on their hearts. (Jeremiah 31:31–33)

> The time is fulfilled, and the kingdom of God has come
> near. (Mark 1:15)

This kingdom is not for Jews alone. The Jews were not selected to be the only objects of divine favour. They were selected for a task, to spread the knowledge and love of God throughout the world. Few Jews have thought that only they would be loved by God, or that the whole world should become Jewish. They have rather thought of Judaism as a witness to the goodness of God in a morally flawed world – a flawed world of which they were part.

To be such a witness requires an acceptance of the divine invitation. Jesus promises that if those who hear him respond to his call they will be empowered and forgiven by the divine Spirit, and will discover a renewal of their divinely given vocation. That is the good news. Jesus may well have been originally speaking specifically to the religious leaders of Judah, and warning them that if they fail in their vocation they will be replaced by "the poor" of Israel. This is in line with his teaching that entrance to the kingdom is not by holding a religious institutional position, or by being conventionally pious, but by obeying the commandments of the heart. And that may be accomplished by those who are not part of any privileged religious group (not even the church, we may now say!).

Luke 14:23 uses the unfortunate expression "compel people to come in" to the feast, which has been used to justify forceful conversion to the church. It should be clear, however, that what is implied is that people should only be compelled by love, and not by force. Anything else would completely contradict the teaching of the Sermon on the Mount.

The Gospel writers, compiling the Gospels after the resurrection and the emergence of a largely Gentile church, probably use this parable in a wider sense, so that Jesus promises all the people of Judah spiritual renewal, but warns that if they reject this invitation their vocation will be extended to a new and more universal, largely Gentile society.

This universal society, which we now know as the church of Christ, was also not selected to be the only object of divine favour. It too is a flawed witness to the goodness of God.

Jesus issues a final invitation to Israel, "I was sent only to the lost sheep of the house of Israel" (Matthew 15:24), and he instructs "the twelve" to "go nowhere among the Gentiles" (Matthew 10:5).

Jesus' mission is to recall the Jews to observance of the *Torah*, to accept the rule of the Spirit before catastrophe envelops the nation. But his disciples felt that they were, after his death, sent to the whole world, to continue in a new way the task of proclaiming the rule of God in every human heart. Between the kingdom of the heart (the kingdom of those in whom the Spirit rules) and the kingdom of heaven (the final completion of God's purpose in a society of true justice and fulfilment) there is the kingdom in history. That kingdom is the people of Israel and it is also the church of the new covenant.

One thing must be carefully guarded against. That is the thought that the Jews have been rejected by God, and wholly replaced by the church (this view is sometimes called "supersessionism"). It is in better accord with the faithfulness of God to say that the first covenant with Israel remains in place. Naturally, Christians will want to say that the Mosaic covenant will be completed by the final revelation to all people of what Christ truly is. That is what Paul's complex argument in Romans 11, which ends with the extraordinary statement, "And so all Israel will be saved" (Romans 11:26), seems to say. But such a full revelation seems to belong to the "new creation", a world beyond the ambiguities and uncertainties of the present world. In this world a new covenant has been added to the Mosaic covenant, so that the vocation of Israel is shared by the largely Gentile church. In a sense, the church extends Judaism to the Gentile world, albeit in a new, less ritual, less juridical, form. There is a new covenant, but it extends and adapts the old covenant, which it does not render obsolete.

The relation between the "old" and the "new" covenants is a complex issue, on which there is continuing theological debate. Christians probably will want to say that ultimately Christ is the saviour of all, Jew and Gentile alike. Yet it is reasonable, and charitable, and consonant with commitment to the love of God for all people, to think that the Mosaic covenant remains a true path to God for the Jewish people. One thing is certain. Whatever we think about that issue, there is no place for anti-Semitism in a church which lives solely by the gift and mercy of God, who in return demands unlimited and universal love.

Divided, imperfect, quarrelsome, and deceitful, both Judaism and the church are shadowed images of eternal beauty intertwined with the ambiguities of earthly pride and power. In both Judaism and the church, those who are invited to belong to the kingdom in history may nevertheless fail to be attentive to the Good and fail to be aware and regretful of their failure to attain it. Matthew, typically, says that they will be bound and cast into outer darkness (Matthew 22:13). It is clear that this is a metaphor, since the unrighteous cannot be thrown both into a furnace of fire and into outer darkness at the same time, nor is it plausible to suppose that there are two different destinations for them.

The fiery furnace stands most aptly for the fires of greed, hatred, and ignorance that destroy human lives. The outer darkness expresses the self-imposed loneliness of exclusion from a society of joy and friendship that one has made oneself incapable of joining because of misery, misanthropy, and suspicion.

We may pray that there will be release from fire and darkness for all who come to regret what they have been and have become. The possibility is virtually stated in Matthew 18:34, "His lord handed him over to be tortured until he should pay his entire debt", and in Luke 12:59, "You will never get out [of prison] until you have paid the very last penny." Here, prison is another metaphor for life after judgment, and these passages imply that debts can be paid.

Though Matthew speaks of the fire, and of weeping and the gnashing of teeth, more than any other Gospel writer, he also says, "It is not the will of your Father in heaven that one of these little ones should be lost" (Matthew 18:14). Even the Gospel editor who speaks more of the judgment of God than any other recognizes that the will of God is that all should know and love God, and that God will seek those who are lost, to bring them back to repentance and love.

The fact will always remain that those excluded from the feast have failed in the vocation to which God invited them. But in the piercing words attributed to Jesus, "Let anyone among you who is without sin be the first to throw a stone" (John 8:7). There is no one who does not need divine forgiveness, and the good news is that such forgiveness is always freely given. This is perhaps the way that the kingdom draws near to us, even as we fail to attain it.

The wicked tenants

A son who refuses to work repents later, while another who says he will work does not do so. It is the first who does his father's will. So it is not those who declare their faith in God (the Pharisees and lawyers) who enter the kingdom, but those who repent, even though they have been swindlers and harlots.

Also, hear of a householder who let out his vineyard to tenants. But when he sent his servants to collect his fruit, they beat and stoned them. When he sent his son, they killed him. So that householder will take away the vineyard and give it to others.

These two thematically related parables (Matthew 21:28–46) are told to the Pharisees, chief priests, and elders in the Temple at Jerusalem. All the Synoptic Gospels record that these religious leaders saw that parables were told against them. Jesus consistently criticizes the guardians and leaders of the prophetic faith. It is they, he says, who persecuted the prophets of the past, and who pay only lip service to God, not honouring him by producing the fruits of kindness, justice, and mercy, but wanting to keep the kingdom for themselves.

According to verse 42 of Matthew's account, Jesus quotes Psalm 118:22, "the stone that the builders rejected has become the chief cornerstone". This plainly relates to Jesus as the foundation stone, but it has a wider resonance (brought out in 1 Peter 2:10, for instance) that those who have been despised and belittled have now become the foundation of the kingdom. Penitent sinners and the poor are given access to the kingdom, while the leading teachers of religion, who have assumed that the kingdom belongs to them, are turned away.

As Jeremias points out, the parable, in the mouth of Jesus, is probably not saying that the kingdom will be taken from the Jews and given to Gentiles. It is saying that the kingdom will be taken from those who lay claim to true religious faith and authority, while in reality pursue fame, honour, and wealth. It will be given to those who make no claim on the kingdom, but who acknowledge their weaknesses and errors, and who work without seeking to possess the fruits of their labours. They work without attachment, out of grateful love, and the kingdom (the clear knowledge of the presence of God, and the full rule of God in their lives) is freely given to them.

What Jesus said to his Jewish hearers applies also to the community of the disciples of Jesus, the church, which in the very first generation became largely Gentile. For the church, the message is the same: swindlers and harlots, if they respond to God's love, enter the kingdom before priests and church dignitaries who flaunt their righteousness and cling to their privileges.

More widely still, perhaps, it is those who produce the fruits of the Spirit (Galatians 5:22), who are not attached to the rewards of their labours, and who have true compassion and love for others, who will share in the love of God. Those who cling to their religion with pride, and react angrily to those who criticize them, will be dispossessed even of what they thought they had. There is judgment, and there is "wailing and the gnashing of teeth". It is not surprising that Jesus aroused anger and opposition from some members of the religious establishment of his day. His words speak just as strongly to members of the Christian churches today.

The field

The kingdom of heaven grows in the hearts of men and women as they become transparent to its power. But in this world the inward work of the Spirit is always mixed with human greed and the will to power, and no one can separate them out. Yet God's purpose of human fulfilment through love and joy is being worked out. There will be a time of separation. Then greed and pride will be burned away, and only love and generosity will remain forever.

This passage (Matthew 13:24–30, 36–43), together with the similar parable of the fishing net filled with good and bad fish (Matthew 13:47–50), could be interpreted as foretelling a future earthly time when good people (children of God) are separated from bad people (children of the devil). The good enter the kingdom and the bad are "thrown into the furnace of fire", where they will weep and gnash their teeth.

There are two main problems with this interpretation. First, it separates good people from bad people much too sharply, when most of us are partly good and partly bad – in fact, mostly bad, as the Sermon on the Mount makes clear. Second, the treatment of the bad seems vindictive and disproportionate. If we are advised to be just and merciful, to love our enemies, to avoid hatred, and to forgive without limit (as we are in Luke 17:4: "If the same person sins against you seven times a day, and turns back to you seven times, and says, 'I repent', you must forgive"), then God cannot be less loving and merciful. Sending someone off to "eternal punishment [*kolasin aiōnion*]" (Matthew 25:46) is not at all loving and merciful. So this interpretation contradicts the general teaching of Jesus in the Sermon on the Mount.

Talk of the kingdom, however, is not about a literal earthly future. It is about an inward and spiritual reality, and about the future triumph of that reality in a "new creation". It is about liberation from evil and sharing in the power of the Spirit.

The first lesson of this passage, then, is that good and evil grow together in the field of the world. This should tell us not to separate good people from bad too sharply and clearly. Most importantly, we should never assume that we are the good and others are the bad. Jesus says, "Do not judge, so that you may not be judged" (Matthew 7:1). We will be judged as we judge others. He recommends that we should never be certain of our own goodness (Luke 18:9–14), but rather depend solely on divine mercy. If that is so, then we should ask mercy for others too.

No ordinary human life is wholly composed of greed and hatred, without a spark of love. And no life is wholly composed of love and generosity, without a speck of greed and egoistic desire. So the separation is not of good people from bad people, but of the good from the bad in every person. For all of us there is burning, as the flames of disordered passion are revealed in all their destructive power. And for all of us there is healing, as the compassionate mind at the heart of being takes us to itself. That is why, although the way to the kingdom is hard and narrow (Matthew 7:14), and few find it in this life, all may take it in the end.

The second lesson of the passage is that there will be a separation of good and evil. The good will be united to God, and the evil will be destroyed. This will not be in an earthly future (that is the literal interpretation). It will be beyond the time of earth.

The good will not literally be gathered into a barn, nor will they literally shine like the sun. All that is good in every human life will be taken into the mind of God, where it will remain forever. There it will be accessible to all who, when their earthly lives have ended, are embraced by the limitless love of God.

The evil will not literally be thrown into a furnace (or a *Gehenna*, a rubbish heap) of fire, where they will still have teeth to gnash and eyes to weep. All that is a cause of evil will be burned away, consumed by its own destructive power. Those who have done evil will weep when they realize what they have done, and may be "saved, but only as through fire" (1 Corinthians 3:15). Perhaps there may be those who refuse to turn from greed and hatred. If so, their destiny is surely destruction, destruction brought about by an ever-increasing hatred that finally turns upon itself in final despair of life. Destruction is, after all, the fate of things thrown onto a fire. But a more charitable interpretation of "throwing out the chaff" is simply that these will not be members of the kingdom, who have eternal life with God. Nothing is said about whether their condition is unchangeable, or about whether God will continue to offer them repentance as long as they exist. The consequences of excluding yourself from the kingdom are sombre and real; but if God is redemptive love, we should hope and pray that those consequences are not final and irreversible, that the excluded will not be condemned to be without redemption for endless time.

The metaphorical fires of the furnace, as Matthew is perhaps rather too fond of pointing out, are eternal (*aiōnios*), or not bound by human time. But what passes through those fires is either purified or destroyed. It is not, as in some interpretations, an endless punishment freely inflicted by God. That cannot be, for if God loves and cares for the well-being even of the enemies of God, and if God forgives all who wish for mercy – and we know these things are true – then such a God will not punish without hope of repentance and release. The news of the kingdom that Jesus brings is good news for all, and especially for "sinners". It is not bad news for the vast majority of people living on earth, whom God has created and whom God will never cease to love.

The third lesson of this passage, then, is that evil is self-destructive, and its full consequences will work themselves out unless evil is renounced. Goodness, likewise, is not something that carries some external reward. When its true nature is allowed to flourish and exist without restriction in its proper form, it is in itself the highest form of happiness and the fulfilment of personal being. The kingdom of heaven is the way of true happiness.

The gospel and the punishment of the unjust

It must be admitted, and indeed openly stated in any honest account, that it is possible to interpret these parables of division and destruction in a very negative way. Matthew's Gospel speaks of "the wrath to come" (Matthew 3:7) and asserts that trees that do not bear fruit will be thrown into the fire (Matthew 3:10). John the Baptist, speaking of the coming of Jesus, speaks of Jesus as the harvester, carrying a flail, separating out wheat from chaff, and throwing away the chaff to be burned (Matthew 3:12).

Gerd Theissen sets out very well a comparison of the Baptist's message with that of Jesus, and points out that in Jesus' preaching "a blunt preaching of judgment… turns into a preaching of grace with the offer of repentance in the face of the judgment which threatens".[10] Nevertheless, Jesus still speaks of a coming judgment in the near future.

It may seem, then, that there is a terrible day of judgment coming soon, and that the vast majority of people will be destroyed in fire. Only a few, the elect, will be spared, and they will have to be both genuinely repentant for their sins and more righteous than the Pharisees. This, however, is hardly a gospel, since it is bad news for the vast majority of people, and may well leave even the faithful few with a nagging doubt about whether they are penitent or good enough to qualify for salvation. Jesus is a fearful judge, and only fervent faith in him can spare his wrath. In some medieval interpretations, only the intercession of Mary (who is apparently more merciful than Jesus) can save us from the judgment of her son.

There is, I think, something wrong with such an interpretation. The gospel is that human sins can be forgiven, that Jesus is the saviour of the world, who gives his life so that those who are lost may be found, and his mission is to social outcasts and sinners. There may be a terrifying judgment. But on the cross Jesus has taken it upon himself: "Christ, having been offered once to bear the sins of many…" (Hebrews 9:28), leaving no sins to be borne by us. Jesus bore our sins; that is, he took upon himself the judgment we deserve. That is good news indeed. Yet we cannot ignore the "bad news" teachings. What, then, are we to make of them?

We must affirm that there is judgment, there is division, and there is destruction. The message of Jesus is not that everything will turn out for the best, whatever people do. But we must, as disciples of Jesus, be very careful to make sure that this bad news does not outweigh the good news of forgiveness and the promise of eternal life. We can best do this by being very careful of where exactly we locate the judgment, division, and destruction.

Human greed, hatred, pride, and lust for power have corrupted the human world and destroyed the lives of millions of people by the gross injustice, exploitation, and violence that are the tragic marks of human history. It is these things that fall under divine judgment, for they have frustrated God's purpose that humans should learn to live together in understanding, kindness, and love.

If we ever come to see our lives as they really are, in the context of God's eternal purpose, we will see our complicity in the failures and corruptions of the world, and we will see the destruction and death that follows from our seemingly small acts of selfishness and greed. To see that clearly, with all its horrific consequences for the world, is already a form of judgment, for it is to see what we could have been and what we have failed to be, and the terrible consequences, both for others and for ourselves, of our failure. If we ever saw that clearly, our problem would be how to go on living with ourselves and with knowledge of the world's tragedy and our failure to deal with it in ourselves and in our daily lives with others. At the very least, it would seem, there would need to be some form of punishment. That punishment would involve coming to see and in some way to feel the harm we have done. It would involve some form of attempted recompense and personal penitential sacrifice, however inadequate that may seem.

The great division is between those who sense something of this tragic failure and those who think that they are somehow immune from it or bear no personal responsibility for it. Jesus' most severe warnings are for the scribes and Pharisees, those who are proud of their religious orthodoxy, yet who love the chief seats in the synagogues and wear fine robes, and who live in style while widows and orphans are neglected. That means, in the contemporary world, that he warns the ministers and priests of the church, who rely on their orthodoxy but neglect the poor, that they are the ones who are condemned, rather than the social outcasts whose lives have been blighted by misfortune and mistreatment for as long as they can recall.

There is a division, but it may not lie where most of us expect. The parable of the sheep and the goats (Matthew 25) makes the division between those who care for the sick and needy and those who do not. It does not make the division between those who have faith in Jesus or believe the right doctrines and those who do not. The implication is that it is the goodness of the heart, and not the orthodoxy of the mind, that is the qualification for entering the kingdom. This is not a conclusion that those who would confine salvation to those who hold correct beliefs (usually, the belief that Jesus is their Lord and saviour, and many other additional beliefs too) have perceived.

Yet this still seems to confine salvation to the few. Jesus said, "The gate is narrow and the road is hard, that leads to life, and there are few who find it" (Matthew 7:14). Many religious believers are in fact excluded from salvation – they cry, "Lord, Lord, did we not prophesy in your name?" but Jesus says, "I never knew you; go away from me" (Matthew 7:22–23). The sheep (the saved) are not those who are filled with faith in Jesus. They are those who practise justice. The narrow way is the way of total commitment to self-giving justice, not a way of hymn-singing and emotional commitment to Jesus. Jesus is in fact presented in the Synoptic Gospels, especially in Matthew's Gospel, as a teacher of the most rigorous moral conduct. The saved will be those who are truly just (very few indeed).

All this avoids an impossibly rigorous moralism only by the fact that, while absolute righteousness is demanded, and few attain it, Jesus came to save sinners, and penitence is accepted where righteousness fails. The point is neatly summed up by the story of the rich man visiting Jesus and refusing to give his goods to the poor. Jesus says, "It is harder for a rich man to enter the kingdom than for a camel to go through the eye of a needle" (that is, it is absolutely impossible). But then Jesus adds that

"for God all things are possible" (Matthew 19:26). As with so many
of Jesus' sayings, this is cryptic and mysterious. On what conditions,
if any, will it become possible for the rich to enter the kingdom? We
are not told. I think the point is that it is humanly impossible, but
divinely possible. That is, humans cannot enter the kingdom by their
own efforts, but only by God's forgiveness and gracious love.

There is destruction, but it is not the destruction of those who,
perhaps through no fault of their own, have never heard of Jesus or
seen what Jesus truly is. It is the destruction of all that makes for
hatred, greed, and pride in every human heart. If we become people
whose lives are centred on those things, then we are on the path to
destruction, to spiritual death.

So, we may say, the gate is narrow that opens onto the kingdom, and
few enter by their own efforts. But with God all things are possible. By
God's power people can enter if they accept God's offer of forgiveness.
If they reject God's power, they remain excluded, condemned by their
own selfishness and greed to lives of misery and anguish.

The possibility of universal salvation

Yet is this not still too exclusive, too cramped and confined a view of
salvation, which leaves most people without hope? Can people who
have never heard of God, or of Jesus, or of God's offer of forgiveness
in Jesus, be saved? The gospel suggests that it is humanly impossible.
But with God all things are possible! That means everything is
possible for God. Therefore God can, if God wills, save everyone
who exists, even if their salvation is humanly impossible, totally
impossible without God.

But does God want to save everyone? If God is revealed in Jesus as a
God of unlimited love, it seems, on grounds of common morality, that
God must so wish. And there is in fact a specific verse to this effect in
the New Testament – not by any means the only one, but a particularly
clear one: "God... who desires everyone to be saved" (1 Timothy 2:4).
That seems definitive. God wants everyone to be saved. We know that
all things are possible for God (Mark 10:27). Therefore God can save
everyone. It is not said that God will save everyone, even those who

have no desire to be saved, who reject love and who reject God with all their hearts. But it is said that God wants everyone to be saved, and that it is possible for God to save everyone.

This is confirmed by 1 John 2:2, "Christ is the atoning sacrifice for our sins, and not for ours only but also for the sins of the whole world." Christ died once, and for all. That is what God wished, and therefore must be possible, even if not absolutely inevitable.

On what conditions will God save everyone? The answer suggested by the Gospels is that God will save those who repent and believe that the kingdom – the power and presence of God – will work in them what they cannot work in themselves, bringing them to final union with the divine love. Are we then back to an exclusive gospel, which condemns most of earth's population just because they have not even heard the Christian gospel? After all, Mark's Gospel ends with the words "the one who does not believe will be condemned" (Mark 16:16). That does sound as if condemnation is the lot of all those who do not positively believe the gospel of Jesus.

The most frequently quoted verse in this regard is from John's Gospel: "I am the Way and the Truth and the Life. No one comes to the Father except through me" (John 14:6). Taken together and in isolation from the rest of the New Testament, these passages sometimes result in the doctrine that all humans (millions and millions of them) are condemned to eternal suffering, except for a tiny few who believe that Jesus is indeed the Son of God who died for their sins. This is a frighteningly vindictive gospel.

Fortunately such an interpretation is in glaring contradiction to the basic gospel message that "God is love" (1 John 4:8). The nature of God's love is spelled out in the Sermon on the Mount, where we are told to "be perfect, as your heavenly Father is perfect" (Matthew 5:48). The Sermon spells out that perfection, and it includes love of enemies (Matthew 5:44) and forgiveness, which is elsewhere said to be without limit (Matthew 18:22). God cannot be less perfect than we are called to be, and so we must believe – and this is indeed good news for most of us – that God loves even God's enemies and forgives them without limit.

Whatever love of enemies is, it is not torturing them in flames forever. It has to include caring for their welfare, never giving up on them, and endlessly seeking to turn them towards life and joy, if at all possible (and all things are possible for God). It is not just those who happen never to have heard of Jesus, it is even those who are enemies of Jesus, that God will continue to love, whose ultimate welfare God will continue to seek, whom God will endeavour to turn toward repentance and acceptance of the divine love into their lives. Perhaps they may resist. Perhaps they may resist forever, for all we know. If they do, then perhaps they do indeed place themselves under condemnation, the condemnation of being excluded, by their own decision, from the kingdom of love and joy. But God, being a God of love, cannot ever cease trying to overcome that resistance for as long as such overcoming remains possible.

This entails that no condemnation needs to last forever. We condemn ourselves by turning from God, but God will never give up on us. There is judgment; there is the pain of loss, of exclusion from the feast of the kingdom; there is the burning of the flames of disordered desire. But there is also the love of God, seeking to turn us to penitence and to fill us with divine life and love. Nothing, not anything in the whole of creation, not even death, can separate us from the love of God that is in Christ Jesus (Romans 8:38–39).

Sheol, the world of the dead, is, of course, one of the things that are part of the whole of creation. Psalm 139:8 makes it explicit, "If I make my bed in *Sheol*, you are there." So even *Sheol* cannot separate us from the love of God. God is present in *Sheol*, and God will be present, not as a judge and torturer, but as one who everlastingly works for the return of the lost sheep that will cause joy in heaven.

The New Testament includes one startling passage that is often overlooked. The first letter of Peter 3:18–20 says that after Jesus died, "he went and made a proclamation to the spirits in prison, who in former times did not obey, when God waited patiently in the days of Noah". Admittedly this passage is very hard to interpret. In medieval thought, it was turned into the harrowing of hell, when Jesus descended to the world of the dead and released the righteous who had been imprisoned until his coming. One modern interpretation is that, as Jesus ascended to heaven, he proclaimed to the fallen angels his victory over evil and death. So we cannot be too confident that one interpretation is correct. Nevertheless, it seems to me that, since Jesus is said to have descended to *Sheol* after his death, those to whom Jesus preached were those who had not obeyed at the time of the flood. If you look back at the Genesis account of the great flood, they were those who were so wicked that every thought of their hearts was evil, and God drowned them. What this passage then says is that God's love did not end with that judgment. It continued, as is shown by the fact that Jesus preached to those who had been condemned for their total wickedness. Jesus did not preach that they were doomed to suffer forever – a gloomy and depressing sermon indeed! According to 1 Peter 4:6, "This is the reason the Gospel was proclaimed even to the dead, so that though they had been judged in the flesh as everyone is judged, they might live in the spirit as God does." Jesus preached, as all evangelists preach, to bring the offer of life and not to affirm the finality of death (see 1 Corinthians 15:22: "as all [*pantes*] die in Adam, so all [*pantes*] will be made alive in Christ"). Even if the passage in 1 Peter 3 does not affirm that Jesus preached to those who had died, this sentence in 1 Peter 4 does seem to say precisely that. The possibility of repentance does not end with death. In fact, it never ends. God stands ready to forgive any and all who repent.

Christ as the way to salvation

What follows, then? I think what follows is that God wants everyone to be saved. From this it follows that God will make it possible for everyone to be saved. And from this it follows that the possibility of salvation cannot depend upon having ever heard of Jesus or of the gospel during earthly life. How, then, does God make salvation possible even for the enemies of God? In the end, Christians say that salvation is through Christ alone. For Christ is the authentic human expression of the eternal love of God, and it is only through the power of God's own love that humans can be brought into union with the divine life. Ultimately, there is no other way. But the path to that ultimate union may be long and winding, and it may begin from many different places, in many diverse historical situations.

The gospel is that God offers, and will continue to offer, to absolutely everyone some beginning of a path that will lead to ultimate salvation. It is completely opposed to the spirit of the gospel to confine salvation to Christians, and it is even worse to confine it to some particular sect of Christians, whether that is the Roman Catholic Church or the born-again separated strict and particular Baptists.

What is that beginning of the path to salvation? We cannot know – remember Jesus' teaching that we should not judge, for we do not know the secrets of human hearts. But we may suppose that God requires the pursuit of a number of things by those on the way to salvation. First, we must be open to the truth as it seems to us to be. Truth must not be distorted by prejudice, hatred, or selective and partial judgments. We must follow our consciences, even if we happen to be objectively in error, though we must also always seek to make our consciences, our moral sense, more sensitive and informed. Second, we must seek to respond to the claims of altruism and benevolence, and turn from selfishness and greed. Third, we must find some liberation from the imperious claims of anger, hatred, passion, and attachment to possessions and pride. We must be selfless and mindful, compassionate and non-attached, and in that way become sensitive to the beauty and wonder of the world. Fourth, knowing the weakness of our hearts, we must be penitent for our failures to seek truth resolutely, to practise altruism genuinely, and to achieve fullness of life. We must be aware of our limitations and failures, as far as we can, and yet resolve to go on with patience, endurance, and hope in facing the challenges our lives bring to us.

None of these things are explicitly religious. It may sound rather odd to say that an atheistic humanist can be saved. It is rather odd, for to be "saved", in the Christian sense, is to know and love God fully and intensely, and to share without restriction the divine life of joy, wisdom, and love. On that definition of salvation, however, hardly anyone is saved during this life. We may believe in God and feel the presence and power of God to some extent, but we should scarcely claim to be filled with God's presence and power. That is for the saints alone, and they are indeed few, and the path to sainthood is hard.

We then, almost all of us, are not yet saved, but we are, we hope, on the path to salvation, to knowing and loving God fully. We may as Christians think that we are securely set on that path, since we know what God is in Christ, and we sense at least some of the love and power of God through the Spirit. Are humanists on the path to salvation too? They may well resent being told so, since they do not think there is a God, and probably would reject God as they understand God (perhaps as a tyrant or heavenly dictator). It is only from a Christian point of view that they could be said to be on such a path. Or perhaps we should not pretend that they are on the same path. They are truly on a different path. Yet that path opens them to the possibility of salvation by a different route.

Christians should resist the temptation to say, "You are on the same path as us, only much further back, and you have a much longer way to go." That does sound arrogant and paternalistic. A less patronizing metaphor may be to accept that paths are genuinely diverse, but to affirm that in the end they will all converge. After all, in the end humanists think that too, but for them all paths converge in death, when the truth at last emerges – though unfortunately it cannot then be known by anyone – that there is no God and no life beyond the grave.

Christians may then say, "We believe there is a God, that Jesus reveals God and the Spirit makes God present to us. Further, the ultimate goal for all humans involves having these beliefs, if they are true, for when we are saved, we will necessarily know what is true." Perhaps we should be careful to add that all present human beliefs, including our own, are inadequate and fallible, and will need to be changed by the final vision of God that we Christians hope awaits all of us. We are all at the beginning of a long journey, and we must all follow the truth as we see it, and seek to be just in ways we think are right. In this world we follow different paths, and they do not all lead, nor are they intended by their adherents to lead, to salvation as conceived by Christians. What we need to stress is that humanists are not condemned by God, or cut off from God. God is working in them, as in everyone, to turn them to the true and the good. If Christians are right, what we will all discover is that the true and the good (the way, the truth, and the life) is God and the wisdom of God, and it may be quite different from what we thought it would be. Yet Christians are bound to believe that they see something genuine of God in Jesus Christ, and that there they find a light that will in the end attract all who do not explicitly reject it.

This is a positive gospel, good news for everyone and not for a favoured few, and good news which does not condemn and exclude, but invites all to greater life and joy. The good news is that God draws near in the person of Jesus to offer the gift of eternal life to all. And that offer really is to everyone without exception. Not all will hear of Jesus, or will understand what he is, but Jesus is not one who limits eternal life to the few who hear and understand him. Jesus is the particular historical pattern on this planet of God's universal action to liberate intelligent beings from anger, greed, and ignorance, and unite them to the divine life of wisdom, compassion, and love. What the life of Jesus shows is not that God loves and redeems only a few lucky individuals. Jesus' life shows that God loves and wishes to redeem every created personal being. His message is not one of condemnation, but of liberation ("God did not send the Son into the world to condemn the world, but in order that the world [*ho kosmos*] might be saved through him", John 3:17). That is the open gospel which Christian churches have by no means always clearly seen, but which they have held in trust for 2,000 years, and which is able to bring new life to the churches today.

The kingdom of God and its fourfold form

The churches of Christ in the history of this world are one form of the kingdom of God. This is a very unfashionable thing to say, as many theologians are reluctant to see the churches as identical to the kingdom in any sense. They perhaps fear that this would give churches too much authority or allow them to claim an unrealistically high standard of morality and wisdom.

However, the parable of the sower implies that some embrace the kingdom and then fall away. The parable of the wedding feast (at least in Matthew 22:11–14) suggests that people "without wedding clothes" can be expelled from the kingdom. The parable of the fishing net explicitly mentions both good and bad fish, and the parable of the wheat and the tares speaks of good and bad growing together. Some distinguish the "kingdom of the Son of man" in Matthew 13:41, in which good and bad both exist, from the "kingdom of the Father" in Matthew 13:43. That seems to me a fairly desperate ploy, and it seems more straightforward to say that there is a historical and ambiguous form of the kingdom on earth, just as the historical kingdom of David – one model from which the gospel idea of the kingdom was derived – was ambiguous. In fact, if we see the ambiguity of the earthly kingdom clearly, this will in itself be the best defence against the temptation to say that any earthly church is totally guaranteed by God to be morally perfect and incapable of error (this is not aimed at the Roman Catholic doctrine of papal infallibility, which is carefully limited in scope, and does not extend to all church teachings).

Within the church, as in the world in general, wheat and tares, good and bad fish, live and grow together. The kingdom on earth is not a society of perfect individuals. The kingdom takes social and historical form as a social reality that grows and develops. In that form, the kingdom is morally and spiritually ambiguous, and in it good and bad are intertwined and inseparable.

The kingdom also exists within human hearts as they are filled with the Spirit of the living Christ. This inner kingdom of the Spirit is not coterminous with any or even with all Christian churches. It is essentially hidden from public view, and its members are known to God alone. In this form of the kingdom also there is ambiguity and failure, for few if any are completely ruled by the Spirit of God. But, unlike institutional churches, the kingdom of the heart at least consists only of those who are sincerely committed to letting the Spirit of God rule in their lives. This is a second form of the kingdom of God.

There is a third form of the kingdom, where there is no evil, and goodness alone exists. That kingdom is not and never will be in this ambiguous and alienated world. It exists, and it exists now, but "in heaven", in the only true reality, in the being of God. It exists now as the saints of God rejoice in the divine presence. The way to enter it is hard, and there are few who find it.

There is a fourth form of the kingdom, which exists at the end of time, and all who do not explicitly and finally turn away from it are to be taken into it as the divine Spirit reconciles to itself and embraces the whole of estranged creation (Ephesians 1:10). This will be the "fulfilment of time", the final realization of the reason for time's existence (the "close of the age [*te sunteleia tou aiōnos*]", Matthew 13:40 and 28:20), the close of the age of our testing, and the entrance into a new age, the age of a fulfilled communion of love.

If these four forms of the kingdom are distinguished, the parables of the kingdom can be interpreted in a coherent and, I think, plausible way. The parables can be seen as speaking, at different times, of the historical kingdom of those who turn ambiguously to the Spirit in the turmoil of the world; the hidden kingdom of the Spirit within human lives; the kingdom in heaven, where Christ in glory now reigns with the blessed few who have passed beyond the world to share in the nature of God; and the kingdom beyond time, when evil will be destroyed and all things will be united in Christ.

If we can see them in this way, these parables can prepare the ground for a philosophical and theological worldview of the sort that I will elaborate on later, especially in the fifth part of this book. What I have called the four forms of the kingdom will become essential features of the creative self-expression of the divine Spirit as it gives itself into the world of finite spirits, draws near to them to liberate them from their estrangement, and raises them to share in the divine nature (2 Peter 1:4).

Summary

This group of parables compares the kingdom of God to seed planted, growing, and bearing fruit; to a rapidly growing community that illuminates the whole of society; to a treasure greater than all others; to a community which seeks to include the lost, the poor, and the outcast; to a feast to which all are invited; and to a vineyard which is taken from those hypocrites who think it is their right and given to those who are truly just and penitent. The kingdom contains good and bad alike, but only the truly just and compassionate really belong to it and will find their final home there.

These parables seem to be about the community of the Spirit with which Jesus is to baptize his disciples. That is the church, in a broad sense that includes all communities of disciples, with all their differences of institutional form. If this is so, the Matthean Jesus would be teaching that the community of his disciples will grow and bear fruit, and that it bears a great treasure – the way to eternal life with God. Its function is not to be the community of the saved, but to enlighten the world in which it exists, to welcome the poor and outcast, to offer life and joy and the unlimited love of God to all without exception.

That is a great ideal, yet in practice these communities will be mixtures of good and bad, and perhaps only a minority of their members will be able authentically to proclaim God's love in word and deed. In his lifetime, Jesus would have been speaking to Jews, calling them to accept the Spirit of God, and reminding them that the way of the Spirit is fully found only by a few. But by the time the Gospels were compiled, this message of God's universal love and of the new community that was to live and proclaim it, the church, had already extended into the Gentile world, where it would continue to grow, ambiguously but surely, to cover the whole earth.

Part 3
The Cosmic Christ
The Eschatological Parables

The second group of parables I will discuss are what may be called the eschatological parables, parables that seem to speak of "the end of the world" or "the end of the age". These parables are the most difficult to interpret, since they use the imagery of Jewish apocalyptic thought – thought about a "day of divine wrath" and the decisive coming of a messianic liberator in glory to found a society of justice and peace. This imagery is alien to us, and often gives rise to literalistic misunderstandings about "the end of the world". For that reason, the imagery needs to be radically reinterpreted in terms of our very different cosmology and worldview.

Wise and foolish bridesmaids
Ten bridesmaids waited for the bridegroom to arrive, but he was delayed. When he came at night, five had oil in their lamps, but five had none, and had to try to find some oil. Meanwhile the bridegroom and the five wise bridesmaids went into the marriage feast, and the door was shut. When the five foolish bridesmaids returned, they were not recognized and could not get into the feast. (Therefore watch, for you do not know when the bridegroom may come.)

This parable (Matthew 25:1–13) is a parable of judgment and division. There is an analogous parable at Luke 13:24–30, where many strive to enter the kingdom by a narrow door, claiming to know the householder. But the householder does not recognize them. These passages also have a thematic connection with the saying about exclusion from the feast of the kingdom (Matthew 8:11–12), where strangers come to sit at table with the patriarchs of Israel, but "the sons of the kingdom" are thrown into "the outer darkness" (Matthew 8:11–12).

There are a number of overlapping strands here, with the common theme that many who expect to share in the marriage feast will not do so. For they are "evildoers" or unready, people who count on their position or their professions of belief in the Lord rather than being committed to true justice and goodness.

The nature of this unreadiness is spelled out in Luke 12:41–46, where the faithful and wise steward is rewarded, while a steward who beats the servants, and eats and gets drunk, is punished. The contrast is between those who do what is right and those who neglect their responsibilities. Many who expect to be "at the feast" will not be there. The feast, then, is for those who are truly just. They will be few, and they will not always be those who regard themselves as just or as otherwise entitled to be honoured guests.

These sayings may seem to be harshly judgmental, and to be distinctly bad news for most people. Taken out of context, they are. But we need to consider by whom they were spoken, and in what context. The speaker is Jesus, who is to give his life to reconcile those who are lost to God. Those to whom he speaks are those who consider themselves to be righteous and to be the religious leaders of Israel, "the sons of the kingdom", the first in the kingdom of God.

True goodness, Jesus says, does not lie in possession of a religious heritage and the keeping of ritual and conventional rules. It lies in befriending social outcasts and having mercy on the poor and weak. Few and rare are those who are truly good. Yet the judge who assesses the righteousness of men and women, and who finds most people wanting, is also the one who journeys into the outer darkness, beyond the joy of the marriage banquet, to seek out all who will turn to him in penitence and grateful love.

So the bridegroom and the householder of these parables is a severe judge who exposes the hypocrisies and self-deceits of human lives. But he is also the good shepherd who gives his life for those who are lost, the father who welcomes the returning prodigal with open arms, and the good Samaritan who binds up the wounds of those who have been broken by life. The magnitude of his self-sacrifice can only be seen when the enormity of human hatred, passion, and greed is seen.

These parables, like the parables of judgment and division that I have already mentioned, can be taken very negatively, as saying that few will be "saved", that God leads many to endless destruction, and that Christ (the householder) will return at any moment to bring a sudden end to human history and shut out the majority of humans from the kingdom forever.

This would be chilling news indeed for most people. The major problem with such a negative interpretation is that it seems wholly at odds with the idea of a loving and compassionate God. Can such a God condemn the vast majority of the world's population to endless suffering, however evil they have been (for even if they are God's enemies, God will never cease to love them)?

That is unthinkable. So there must be a different interpretation of Jesus' words. There is. It is not hard to find. Jesus is speaking to those who consider themselves "sons of the kingdom", but are angry, selfish, deceitful, and vindictive. He warns them that goodness is not an easy path, and very few manage to be truly good. The kingdom which they expect as their right will be given to others (Matthew 21:43), and their way of life will be exposed for what it already is – a way of darkness, misery, and destruction. If they wish to enter the kingdom, his hearers must "repent" – acknowledge their moral failures – and rely solely on the mercy of God for their spiritual health and fulfilment (that is what "salvation" truly means).

To put it in a nutshell, Jesus is not primarily predicting future physical events. He is saying that there will be judgment in the world to come, and that it will be a serious matter of exclusion from joy and self-induced torment. But he is also disclosing present spiritual states. You may think you are secure with God because of your membership of some religious tradition – and that means that it is now members of Christian churches, not long-dead "scribes and Pharisees", to whom his words are addressed. But being a paid-up "son of the kingdom" is not what matters. God requires love of goodness for its own sake – "purity of heart" – and that is almost impossible to achieve.

Yet, as I have suggested, even this is too moralistic for the Christian gospel, which is a gospel of mercy and forgiveness. God loves everyone with an unlimited and unending love. And God desires that history will be fulfilled when it has run its course, not simply ended at some arbitrary and unexpected moment ("He has made known to us the mystery of his will… as a plan for the fullness of time, to gather up all things in him, things in heaven and things on earth", Ephesians 1:9–10). These are the basic axioms of the positive gospel. They must provide the main clue to interpreting the parables.

So, though most people will miss the mark of goodness, and though the evil that they do must bring them to the "outer darkness" of loneliness, regret, and lovelessness, their exclusion need not be final. God's love will never change, and will continue to offer life to all who will accept it.

Why do these parables then sometimes seem so judgmental and moralistic? I think it is because Jesus is speaking to people who think they are pious and good, to show them that they are in sin as much as people they regard as notorious sinners, and that the kingdom is not theirs by right. Few can be saved by their own moral holiness. Jesus' answer to the question, "Who can be saved?" is not in the end that few will be saved. It is that what is impossible for mortals is possible for God (Luke 18:27). Salvation is by God's grace alone, which frees us from darkness and fire. The verbal threat of destruction is offset by the personal presence of the saviour of the world, and the severity of Jesus' moral teaching is balanced by the self-giving compassion of the one who came not to condemn, but that "the world might be saved through him" (John 3:17).

True, according to John those who do not believe are said to be condemned already. But "this is the judgement, that the light has come into the world, and people loved darkness rather than light" (John 3:19). People condemn themselves by their love of darkness, but it is now possible to turn towards the light. The possibility of belief, of accepting light when it is rightly seen, is never closed by a God whose love cannot be defeated by any future event, or by death itself. Jesus' message, then, is that we do indeed virtually all fall short of what God requires, and cannot by our own efforts gain union with the divine life. The patriarchs of Israel certainly fell short, if the biblical accounts of their lives are to be believed. It has to be said, then (and Paul does say it, in the fourth chapter of his letter to the Romans), that they too are saved by God's grace, not by their own efforts. God forgives and unites to the divine life all who turn to him, now or at any time. Jesus issues a call for acceptance of the renewing Spirit of God and the assurance that the Spirit draws near in him. In these parables, we need to see what is not said, the presence of the one who speaks, who warns of severe judgment, but who is to take that judgment on himself.

It is very easy to misinterpret biblical passages if they are taken out of context. Some of the Gospel parables, though I see little reason to deny that they reflect fairly accurately what Jesus said, can easily be interpreted as judgmental and moralistic, requiring unrealistically high moral standards and threatening destruction for all who do not obey. Or, if such moralism is mitigated by a doctrine of salvation by faith, they can still be interpreted as arbitrarily exclusive, condemning all who do not overtly accept Jesus as their saviour. But there is a third choice: they can be taken in the light of an even wider perspective of salvation through grace, stressing the universal and unlimited will of God for human salvation, disclosed in and through Jesus, which does require repentance and trust, but places no time limit or other barrier on the possibility of faith.

I have suggested that these parables disclose the spiritual standing of persons before God rather than predict the occurrence of physical events in the near future. Yet it seems clear there is also a future reference in the parables. The spiritual state of human hearts is now hidden, but it will be fully disclosed. There will be a feast for those who are fully conscious of the presence of God, and there will be outer darkness and the fires of *Gehenna* for those who choose the way of selfish desire. These may not be physical feasts and fires, but they are real future states into which men and women can enter.

Those who accept the positive gospel will hope and pray that none will actually be thrown into the outer darkness forever (perhaps we would not want even a feast to go on forever without a break!). A clearer realization of the possibility of exclusion might in the end be sufficient to bring people to repentance. That is why these are not predictions, but warnings. The spiritual future God desires is that evil will be destroyed, and all will live with God – though God would not compel people to return love against their will.

The complete destruction of evil and the existence of a society of perfected human lives will be beyond history. There are, nevertheless, anticipations of these spiritual outcomes within history. Jesus taught that the Temple, and the age of the Temple sacrifices, would be brought to a savage end. The kingdom would be taken from the high priests and the Pharisees (but probably not from the Jewish people as such) and extended to cover the Gentile world. Christ would reign at the right hand of God, and the age of a renewed humanity truly united to God would begin.

Just as in the classical prophecies of the great Jewish prophets, history will not be as cosmically cataclysmic as the texts overtly state. But historical events will show destruction, judgment, and renewal in a way which anticipates the end of time, when evil is finally judged and destroyed, and all of humanity which does not wilfully and knowingly resist will be renewed.

If we consider the nature of Old Testament prophecy, and the ways in which such prophecies were fulfilled; if we consider the New Testament teaching in the letters of the early churches of salvation by grace; and if we consider the nature of Jesus' parables as cryptic, symbolic, hidden yet powerful messages of spiritual awakening for those who had "eyes to see and ears to hear"; then we will not see the words of Jesus simply as condemnations of "a sinful and adulterous generation". We will see them as exposures of spiritual bankruptcy indeed, and as warnings of what human lives will be if they continue on their present course. But they are also, and primarily, invitations to accept the rule of the forgiving love of God, which was drawing near in Jesus' own person, and which would never cease to draw near in the continuing presence of the Spirit to all who were ready to accept.

Parables of judgment provide an anticipation of what the world is like, and of what human lives will be like, without the redemptive love of God. But the messiah is not one who leaves the world to its self-inflicted agony. He is the redeemer of the world, and no one is ever beyond the reach of his love – except those, if there are those, who reject the reality of love itself (they are those, perhaps, who "blaspheme against the Holy Spirit" and "will not be forgiven, either in this age or in the age to come", Matthew 12:31–32). They will not be forgiven, not because God obstinately refuses to forgive them, but because they themselves refuse to repent and turn to God, to accept the love that God unceasingly offers to them. Nevertheless, if their hearts soften and they repent, God's forgiveness will always be offered to them. No one is irretrievably condemned, except those who condemn themselves by turning away from love.

Creation and consummation: The beginning and end of time

It may be helpful to make a comparison between the Christian doctrine of creation and the doctrine of a final judgment day. John Robinson did this in a rather neglected but significant book, *In the End, God*, and it has always seemed to me that the comparison is an illuminating one. If we make such a comparison, we may see that judgment is not an event which only comes towards the end of human history, just as creation was not an event that only took place at the beginning of human history.

Creation is the relation of every moment of time to the eternal reality of God which is beyond all times. The Genesis stories of creation use the symbols of a garden of bliss, a human figure (Adam) who stands for all humanity, a God who walks in the garden, and "days" to represent epochs of cosmic history. They do not tell what literally happened at the beginning of history. But they represent the absolute dependence of all things upon God, and the calling of humans to be stewards of the earth.

So stories of a final judgment and the return of the Son of man in glory do not tell what will literally happen at the end of history. There is no literal throne, no figure standing on the clouds, and no single day on which every human being lines up before the throne, or on which some of them are suddenly pulled up into the clouds. These symbols represent the final goal of all things in God, the fact that the moral acts of human beings will have serious consequences for the agents, and that God's purpose is that all should ultimately share in the divine life.

Just as creation is the relation of every moment of time to God, so judgment is the relation of every moment of time to the eternal reality of God which is beyond all times. In every moment of time the Christian disciple can discern a threefold dynamic. First there is the fact that the origin of all times is in God. Good and evil alike arise from God, though God positively intends and wills only the good, while the existence of some evil and the potentiality for greater evil arises with the good by necessity. All times arise from God and depend wholly on God, though God wills the good to be retained and nourished, while the evil is to be transformed and overcome wherever that is possible. This first aspect is creation.

The second aspect of every time, at least in human history, lies in the way in which humans receive and appropriate each time as it comes. A moment of time can be celebrated and savoured, it can be patiently endured, or it can be used to contribute towards a future good. But a moment of time can also be a moment of self-centred gratification, of embittered resentment, or of destructive conflict with others. This aspect is the moment of freedom.

The third aspect of every time is God's reception of time into the divine life. God can incorporate moments of time into the divine experience of appreciation and joy, God can reject and exclude moments which would bring suffering and division into the divine life, and God can transform or redeem moments by placing them within wider patterns of goodness towards which they can contribute significantly.

This third aspect is judgment. Pictures and parables of judgment depict the acceptance, rejection, or redemption of each moment of time as an aspect of the eternal life of God. In the terms of the parable of the bridesmaids, the wise bridesmaids are accepted – and those who are accepted in this way, because of the outstanding sanctity of their lives, are few. The foolish are rejected – and they may include many who were confident of their place with God. But there is a third possibility. The foolish bridesmaids may yet be redeemed – that possibility is not stated, but silently expressed in the life of the one who utters the parable, and who draws near in person even to those whom he warns of rejection.

So when we are told that we do not know the day or hour when the bridegroom or householder may come, a natural way to take this is to say that we must watch at every time (just as we must accept our creation, our total dependence upon God, anew at every time). To believe in creation is to accept every time from God as a new creation. To believe in the fulfilment of the kingdom is to surrender every time to God and to accept the rule of the Spirit which forgives, purifies, and redeems. For God does accept or reject our lives into the divine life at every moment. We are judged at every time, and rejected or redeemed at every time, and the kingdom (the presence of God) is present at every time. The reason we must be prepared for the coming of the Lord at any time is that the Lord actually comes at every time, though that coming is often not clear to us.

At no historical time is the kingdom present in its fullness, when all evil is eliminated and we love naturally and freely, rejoicing in the presence of God. Rather, we live in a darkened and estranged world, where corruption and hatred are rife, and where the presence of the kingdom is hidden and elusive. Thus on the one hand we hope that time will not end – for it offers the opportunity for new forms of beauty and goodness and for new generations of people who can create and appreciate them. Yet on the other hand we also hope for the end of time, when we will see and know the fulfilment of all things in God, and where tears and sorrow will be no more.

Those who follow Jesus live between the tension of these two hopes. We pray that all the good possibilities that God wills for the world, and all the good that we can contribute to the world, may have time to grow and flourish. But we also pray that we will know Christ in glory, the end of evil, and the final flourishing of all things in God.

The imagery of the Old Testament

Those who heard Jesus teach saw things very differently from how we do. For some of them the kingdom of God would be established by the liberation of Judah from Roman domination, the keeping of the *Torah* with full rigour, and the return of the lost tribes to Jerusalem. From the modern perspective, that was a small-scale and rather nationalistic vision. The rest of the world played a relatively small role, and the "new age", the fulfilment of prophetic dreams, would be sufficiently realized by a new and vibrant sociopolitical life for Judah.

I do not suppose that the standard images of a coming on the clouds with angels and trumpet calls were taken literally by those who understood the gospel of Jesus. In the prophetic books of the Hebrew Bible, such symbols represented the fall of oppressive political powers (like Babylon or Persia), and the renewal of Jewish life centred on Jerusalem and the keeping of the *Torah*. For instance, the image of the darkening of sun and moon and the fall of the stars from the sky is taken from Isaiah 13:10. There it is part of an oracular utterance explicitly named as "the oracle concerning Babylon" (Isaiah 13:1). It is a foretelling of the future fall of Babylon, and its cosmic imagery was not meant to be taken literally. In the Gospels, the probable reference of such imagery is to the fall of the Roman Empire.

Similarly in Old Testament apocalyptic thought, the "Son of man" (Daniel 7:13–14) is the true Israel, the clouds represent the *Shekinah*, the presence of God, and the gathering of the elect is the return of the twelve tribes from the corners of the earth to Jerusalem (see the next section for more on this). The corresponding reference in the New Testament, heavily disguised from curious Roman eyes by traditional symbolism, is very probably to the fall of Rome, together with the destruction of the Temple in Jerusalem, and the renewal of the covenant in a new form.

These were commonplace prophetic themes and symbols, and we might expect that Jesus would have used them to convey his message. But his message carried overtones – also present in the writings of the major prophets – that were politically and religiously explosive.

The judgment would fall not only on Rome but on the religious leaders of Israel. Perhaps the "new age" would not be a renewed Jewish community, but a new and more universal sort of covenant between God and humanity. And that covenant would be an inward and spiritual covenant, not one with a visible and politically dominant institution.

Part of the apparent severity of the judgment parables can be better understood by placing them in this context. Jesus was challenging the Jewish political scenario, and warning that things might well turn out in ways that the religious leaders of Israel did not expect. It might be the religious leaders, not the Romans, who would be judged by being overthrown and destroyed. Jesus was proclaiming a "last chance" opportunity for the Judaeans to avoid such a fate. And perhaps he was pointing out that God's kingdom might come in a new and non-political form, even if the fate of Jerusalem was sealed. These were teachings that would have been anathema to the political and religious authorities of the day, throwing doubt on their legitimate authority and warning that it was about to end. It is not wholly surprising that they conspired against Jesus and eventually had him crucified.

But they misunderstood the message of Jesus. He might indeed be king, but not in a political sense – "my kingdom is not from [ek tou] this world" (John 18:36). It is not authorized by anything in this world, and it does not belong to this world. I think it is plausible to see Jesus as teaching that the kingdom would come on earth in a new form, a spiritual form that was no longer wedded to the political hopes of Israel and Judah. In that case, Jesus' challenge to the high priests and Pharisees was to recognize this possibility, and accept the inward and spiritual nature of the covenant kingdom. But he found his disciples mostly among the poor and powerless. He foresaw the destruction of Judah and the Temple. And I do not think it is implausible to suppose that he looked for a new community of the spirit of the love of God that would arise from the ashes of Jerusalem and spread the good news of the redeeming love of God throughout the whole world. Whether or not he did so, by the time the Gospels were written this had become an implication of his life, death, and resurrection that put his teachings in a new light.

The fig tree without fruit

Fig trees without fruit will be cut down. They have one more year to make it.

This parable (Luke 13:6–9) may be the origin of the story of Jesus
cursing the fig tree without fruit in Matthew 21:18–19 and Mark
11:12–14. It is short and to the point. It carries a note of warning,
and is part of the prophetic teaching of Jesus that a day of crisis for
Judah is at hand. There were many movements of national revival and
opposition to Roman imperialism at the time of Jesus. Jesus warns
that unless such movements are founded first on spiritual renewal,
they will end in disaster – as they did, in AD 70, when the Temple
was destroyed, and in AD 135, when Judah was annihilated by Roman
armies. As Jesus spoke, Judah was in the last days of the age of the
second Temple, and that age would end in darkness and destruction
unless there was a return to the true spirituality of the kingdom. If
Jesus' message was not heard, the "end of the age" would be one of
judgment and catastrophe.

   Yet even if that were so, from it would spring a new age and a new
spiritual order – symbolized by the rule of the "Son of man", the
one whose true humanity was fulfilled by union with the life of the
eternal God, and whose rule would be not political and national, but
spiritual and universal. So, in Jesus' use of apocalyptic imagery, the
themes of judgment and of hope and renewal are inextricably linked
together. This is emphasized in another fig tree parable, from Mark
13:28–29.

The parable of the fig tree

*When leaves appear on the fig tree you know that summer is near. So when you
see the "signs of the times" you know that he* [in Luke 21:31, "the kingdom of
God"] *is near.*

There can be no doubt that many early Christians (like many modern
Christians) thought that Christ would come in glory within their
lifetimes (cf. 1 Thessalonians 4:15–16, the earliest New Testament

document we have: "For this we declare to you by the word of the Lord, that we who are alive, who are left until the coming of the Lord, will by no means precede those who have died").

The point of Paul's remark is, I think, to assure his readers that the faithful dead live with Christ and that his readers will meet them again. That is what Paul believed Jesus himself had taught. Paul's particular belief at this stage seems to have been that the faithful dead "sleep in Jesus". Perhaps they are in an "intermediate state", in *Sheol* or in Paradise, and are then raised "bodily" at a specific time when Christ appears in the clouds, and the faithful living are caught up into the clouds to meet them.

It is hard to know whether Paul thought of this literally, or whether he was using symbols familiar from the Old Testament to affirm that the dead would be raised to life again, and that they and present believers would be united in Christ, in the *Shekinah*, the cloud of the divine presence, in some way that was not literally imaginable. Since Paul was quite a sophisticated scholar (according to Acts, a pupil of Gamaliel), I think it more likely that he was using symbolic language to convey belief in resurrection and the reunion of all believers in Christ. But Paul at this stage does seem to have thought that this would bring an end to human history and would occur within his lifetime. By the time he wrote the letter to the Romans, he seems to have changed his mind: "A hardening has come upon part of Israel, until the full number of the Gentiles has come in" (Romans 11:25). This implies quite a long time during which the gospel will be preached to the Gentiles. The extreme literalist view of a return within a generation has begun to be modified. Other writers (like the author and the redactor of John's Gospel) modified it even more, and in time it was quietly dropped by much of the later church.

Nevertheless, an early end to human history is probably what Paul taught to the young churches he founded at this early time in his Christian life. But whatever Paul thought, while Jesus almost certainly did teach that there is life beyond death and that Paradise is communal rather than solitary and individual, it seems to me highly doubtful that Jesus taught that he would literally return on the clouds taking the faithful living and the newly resurrected dead to be with him there.

My reasons for this view are as follows: Jesus taught that God is "the God not of the dead, but of the living" (Luke 20:38). His parable of the rich man and Lazarus assumes that the dead are conscious in either *Sheol* or Paradise (or in Abraham's bosom). On the cross, he promises the penitent thief that he will be with him that day in Paradise. He is said to have spoken with Moses and Elijah in a vision. According to Matthew, he said that the dead in outer darkness or the fire weep and gnash their teeth, while the righteous have a great feast. These statements do not suggest that the dead are asleep until the resurrection. Neither do they give a literal description of how the dead exist.

Jesus' talk of the coming of the Son of man on the clouds, and even his choice of the expression "Son of man", are echoes of Old Testament symbols that are not literal, so it is very doubtful whether he would have meant such statements to be taken literally.

There has been immense scholarly controversy about what the phrase "Son of man" could have meant, or even whether Jesus could possibly have applied it to himself. The obvious reference is to Daniel 7:13–14, where in a vision the prophet sees one "like a son of man [a human being]" coming with the clouds of heaven and being present to the "Ancient of Days". The "one like a man" is given dominion over all peoples and nations, and his kingship will never be destroyed.

This person appears after a succession of animal forms, four great beasts, all clearly mythical and visionary, have appeared in a dream to the prophet. A lion, a bear, a panther, and a terrible unnamed monster are generally thought to be symbols for the Medes, Persians, Babylonians, and Syrians. They are followed by one like a human being, who almost certainly represents the true Israel, a truly human as opposed to a bestial king, whose dominion will cover the earth forever.

The prophet predicts that imperial tyrannies will be destroyed, and a truly humane society will come to be. Tragically, this has never decisively happened in political or historical reality, though all tyrannies do eventually pass away, and the work of faithful love endures. Nevertheless the teaching of Jesus, standing in the prophetic tradition, seems to be that all tyrannical systems of power can be overcome by love. There can be partial gains in history, but we must look for final victory beyond history, when the often hidden choices of human hearts will be revealed for what they truly are. There will be judgment, there will be victory, and there will be redemption. The practical message is that we must live in commitment and in hope – as though "the householder will return at any time", and as though we will see the kingdom fully realized.

In the Synoptic Gospels, Jesus refers to himself not as "Son of God", but as "Son of man". If he had in mind the Daniel vision, he would be claiming to represent a truly humane kingdom that would succeed and overthrow the military dictatorship of worldly empires – especially, in this case, of Rome. I think this is strongly suggestive of the idea that the kingdom of God would be a spiritual, inward kingdom as opposed to a political, imperial rule. Jesus could have seen himself as the inaugurator and ruler of such a spiritual community, which would be the true Israel as opposed to the "fallen" Israel represented by the high priests and Pharisees.

Geza Vermes argues that the phrase "Son of man" (from the Aramaic *bar-nasha*) cannot be used as a title referring to a specific figure, like some heavenly being, for example. It could, even though rarely, be used as a circumlocution for "I, the human being who is speaking". In that case, Jesus' references to the "Son of man" are references to himself, and he can be seen as referring to himself in his representative role as the truly human king of Israel, who would be vindicated in the near future, when he would take up his rule ("appear in the glory of the Father").

When would the Son of man take up his rule? When would the kingdom come? Matthew 24:33 and Mark 13:29 both speak of Jesus or "the harvest" being "at the very gates" when the signs of the times are seen, whereas Luke makes the same point by saying that "the kingdom of God is near" (Luke 21:31). The exact day and hour are not known, but it would be very soon, and before all those who heard Jesus teach had died (Luke 21:32).

I am not trying to construct a clear and definitive conceptual straitjacket into which to force the complex set of diverse metaphorical

images in the New Testament. My aim is the relatively modest one of
seeing if there is a coherent and plausible theology of "the end of the
age" that takes the images seriously, but interprets them in the light of
our contemporary understanding of history and the cosmos. Thus in
what is admittedly a reading back into the text of later interpretations
of a wide range of biblical materials, I think that these statements
can make good sense if we suppose that the Son of man ascended the
throne when he died and that he was then raised by God to heaven or
Paradise, to rule in heaven forever. There he would be the Lord of all
who lived the liberated life of the kingdom of the heart. He would be
Lord of all who, though they had fallen short of such a life, yet turned
to him in penitence and grateful love. He would be king of the Jews, of
all Israelites who looked for and embraced the rule of God. He would
also be Lord of the church, the ambiguous but covenanted community
that was to take the gospel of the Spirit throughout the world. He
would be the Lord of Paradise, reigning with the saints in glory. And
he would be the Lord of the final Judgment, taking upon himself the
sins of all who fall under condemnation, and opening the way for all
who accept him to share in the life of God.

On this reading, the Son of man begins his kingly rule when Jesus
ascends to heaven. This is what I have called the third form of the
kingdom. It is the spiritual realm where the saints live consciously in
the presence of God, and where Christ began his rule after his ascension.
There are indeed few who take the narrow path to this kingdom, the
Paradise that Jesus promised to the penitent thief. But they, we may
suppose, continually pray for those, living and dead, whom God calls
into the kingdom, when they have been "purified by fire", assisted by
the prayers of the saints, and sanctified by the Spirit of God.

When, as the Gospels claim, Jesus accepted the titles of bridegroom,
king, and messiah, it was in view of his calling to reign in the human
afterworld, not in any belief that he would become a political ruler in
the imminent future of this world. In applying imagery taken from
the prophet Daniel to himself he was applying imagery based on a
series of visionary dreams, not a set of literal predictions. Thus the
kingdom of the Son of man comes with the resurrection and exaltation

of Jesus, though it comes in a spiritual rather than a historical and political sense.

Yet there is a historical dimension to the kingdom. According to Luke, when Jesus was asked when the kingdom of God was coming, he said: "The kingdom of God is not coming with things that can be observed… for in fact, the kingdom of God is within [*entos*] you" (Luke 17:20–21). Many commentators translate *entos* as "among", and the word can bear both meanings. Whichever translation you choose, the kingdom is present, and it is not visible. It is not an observable future event, as a literal appearance on clouds most certainly would be. It is known in the hearts of men and women, and in the community in which the Spirit of God rules. On this view, the coming of the kingdom on earth may correspond to the coming of the Holy Spirit with power at Pentecost. That is when the rule of Christ, established in heaven, is made manifest on earth, when what I called the first and second forms of the kingdom, the rule of Christ as Lord of the church, and the rule of the Spirit of Christ in human lives, begins. The rule of Christ had already begun in a sense as people encountered the person of Jesus, but only after Jesus' death and resurrection, at Pentecost, did it come openly and with power. The fourth and final form of the kingdom will only exist at the end of historical time, when all that is good in this creation will be gathered into God's new creation.

The Son of man will not exist physically in the future in any specific place on this earth. Luke's Gospel says, "As the lightning flashes and lights up the sky from one side to the other, so will the Son of man be in his day" (Luke 17:24). Is that not a visible sign? If it were, it would contradict the immediately preceding passage in Luke, which denies that the kingdom comes with observable events. The lightning flash cannot be a visible, literal, flash. What does it symbolize? Just as symbols of the darkening of sun and moon and the fall of the stars from heaven were, in the Old Testament, speaking of the fall of the military powers of the world, so the lightning flash "in heaven" represents a change in the world historical order. The lightning flash joins earth to heaven and begins a new world order as it illuminates the whole world. Henceforth, Christ, the Son of man who is "the visible image of the invisible God", and who rules in heaven, is present spiritually everywhere in the world, and can be discovered at any place, though always hidden within the heart.

But was there not an early Christian belief that Christ would return in glory very soon? His coming with power in the descent of the Spirit is a critical event, but it is not the return of Christ in glory. It seems likely that some early Christians ran together the destruction of Jerusalem and the consequent end of the age of the Judaic priesthood and the Temple sacrifices; the birth of the church, the new covenant community; the ascent of Christ to "the right hand of God"; and the final coming of the kingdom at the end of time. The oral traditions that had been passed on from the apostles were reshaped around these themes, and it was quite easy to take parables about the end of Temple religion and the spiritual enthronement of Jesus, and make them apply to the end of history.

In an important sense this was correct, though the end of history was not to occur in the near future. It is important to see the double meaning of "end" when speaking of the end of time. "End" means both the finish, the termination of time, and the fulfilment, the goal, the completion, of time. At the End, time is both negated – in the historical form in which we experience it, it is abolished – and fulfilled, for there is a different and more positive form of time that awaits.

That form of time is one where the past is not lost, where the present is not a fleeting and transient moment that can never be fully grasped, and where the future is not an unknown or threatening prospect. There will be time of a sort, for there will be change, creativity, growth, and relationship. But it will be time without loss and beyond the anxiety of undetermined freedom. All historical times will be present, though they will be transfigured by the presence of God, which forgives and heals the hurts of the past, and fulfils and completes the capacities and possibilities that could not be realized in the relentless onrush of historical time.

The end of historical time is a new age, but not another age like this one, or a simple continuation of this one. Each historical time will be present, though transfigured, so that the End is both now and yet to come, and the present can be, to use Pannenberg's term, a prolepsis (a prefiguration or anticipation) of the End in which it will be transfigured and fulfilled. That is, the present prefigures and anticipates the End, and in that sense the End is regarded as a present reality. To understand the symbolism of the return of the Son of man in glory is to see that every present moment is fulfilled in Christ, and to see each moment in the light of that disclosure of its true meaning. Then we can truly say, "Come, Lord Jesus", and pray that this time will not be forever lost, but will be completed when Christ is fully known, and all times are made one and reconciled by participation in him.

It is not surprising that some disciples believed that historical time really would end in their generation. Their hope for the kingdom was centred on the restoration of Israel, and the rest of the world was peripheral to their outlook. The world had only existed a countable number of generations from Adam, and no radical improvement or change was to be expected in history. So it would, from their point of view, be better if history ended with judgment on the Gentiles and the restoration of the Davidic monarchy in Jerusalem. Had not Jesus appointed the apostles as judges of the twelve tribes, and promised that the Temple would be rebuilt? And had he not been raised from death, thereby beginning the anticipated resurrection of the dead?

In believing this, however, they overlooked many things about Jesus' teaching. He had indeed, he said, only come to call Israel to repentance or, if that failed, to face a devastating catastrophe. But his central message of the love of God for all people had implicitly looked toward the inclusion of the Gentiles in the kingdom. If the accounts of the great resurrection commission to preach the gospel to all the world are reliable, then he explicitly extended the kingdom far beyond the bounds of Israel. And had he not stated that the kingdom would be taken from those who expected that it was theirs, and opened to others? The gospel cannot be limited in space to one small Mediterranean principality, and it cannot be limited in time to one generation after Jesus. So the churches came to see that many peoples and many generations must be touched by the gospel. Paul came to see that the appearing of Christ in the glory that was truly his would only come when the full number of the Gentiles had been reached.

And that is not yet the end. For we know, as they could never have known, that there are stars and galaxies by the million, and that time will not end until they have all run their course, with whatever life forms they may sustain. The whole of creation will be taken to participate in God. And now the glorious appearing of Christ, which the letters to the Ephesians and Colossians depict as including the whole cosmos, seems to be indefinitely deferred.

For that reason the Christian hope for the coming (the *parousia*, the being present) of Christ does not refer simply to the end of time. It refers to each moment of lives that are touched by grace as a prolepsis of the End of times. When we see that, we see the inadequacy of millenarianism, which looks only for better worldly things in a near future. Rather, the whole of worldly time must be transfigured into the time of God. That will be both the judgment and the redemption of time, and so each moment may be seen as a confrontation with Christ.

The great division

The coming of the Son of man will be like Noah's flood, or like the destruction of Sodom, in which all perished. On that day, do not turn back to collect your belongings. In that night there will be two together; one will be taken and the other left.

Luke 17:26–36 is a parable of destruction and division. The Son of man is clearly Jesus, for he is to suffer and be rejected. On a literal reading of the parable, when he appears again, there will be destruction and terror for all who are not saved by the Lord.

Some have thought of this as a cataclysmic divine intervention in history, an unmistakeable unveiling of the glory of the Son of man, when the unrighteous would perish and the righteous would be taken to the presence of the Lord.

There are three main problems with this literal interpretation of the text. First, it is brutally vindictive, promising a terrifying death for huge numbers of people. This is a problem because it is in marked tension with Jesus' recorded teaching that God is loving and compassionate to all.

Second, it takes Noah's flood, Sodom's destruction, and the coming of the Son of man literally, as public events in history. The problem here is that many people, including me, take the stories of the flood and the destruction of Sodom as half-remembered catastrophic natural events, which have been given a rather unappealing interpretation as acts of a vengeful God. The stories give a very primitive and indeed unacceptable picture of what God is really like, compared with Jesus' picture of a loving Father.

Moreover, Luke himself says that the kingdom is "within" or "between", and in any case not an external event. In the Old Testament the Son of man is not a person, but a symbol in a dream recorded in the seventh chapter of the prophetic book of Daniel. This suggests that the "revelation of the Son of man" is not a public event at all, but a symbol of the replacement of military dictatorship by a humane and compassionate political order. In a further twist to the Old Testament picture, Jesus rejected any political role. So the symbol rather speaks to me of the birth of a new community of the spirit of love.

This would be the opposite of the appearing of a vengeful Son, destroying his enemies. It would be the ending of the old order of vengeance, of military oppression, and religious hypocrisy, and the appearing of a community empowered by the self-giving Spirit of God. Those who look back to the old order ("Lot's wife") are left to the destruction that self-obsession brings, while those who look to the suffering and redeeming Son (who do not cling to their old lives) are taken to be with him forever. The inclusion by Luke in this short passage of the saying about Lot's wife and of Jesus' saying that "whoever seeks to gain his life will lose it" seems to support this interpretation.

The third problem is that the parable as it stands is just too myopic. It stands wholly within the Jewish tradition, without regard to the rest of the world or of history. We must recontextualize Jesus, so that he becomes not the one who is to bring history to an end in the near future, but the origin of a new religious community with a new idea of God and of God's purpose for creation. The new community of the Spirit is a community of love and of service to others, not an organization consisting of those who are saved while everyone else in the world perishes. The new idea of God is that God desires the welfare of all creatures without exception, and is not a wrathful and vindictive tyrant. The new idea of God's purpose is that God enters into the suffering and alienation of the human world in order to unite all rational creatures to the divine life, so that they may know God and enjoy him forever.

So we might reconstrue the saying like this: when the new community of love appears, the world will be revealed as a self-destructive and doomed enterprise of alienated human wills. We can be liberated from this world by turning to the God of love revealed in Jesus. If we do so, he will take us to himself forever. And (what is left unstated in the parable, but is manifest in the life and nature of Jesus) the path of liberation, the way to salvation, is never closed, even by death.

Did Luke construe it like that? He may have retained traces of belief in the vindictive wrath of God – even though his own recounted parables of the prodigal son and the good Samaritan should have abolished such traces completely. And he possibly shared the myopic view of history which expected the return of Christ to end history fairly soon.

Did Jesus think like that? We cannot know for sure. But I believe the record shows that Jesus taught that we must oppose in ourselves everything that is in the slightest degree vindictive. His own sayings, so highly paradoxical and counter-intuitive (just remember, "If your right eye causes you to sin, tear it out and throw it away", Matthew 5:29!), show a skilled and consistent use of metaphor and hyperbole that counts strongly against literal interpretations of his sayings. And though he saw his own mission as only to Israel, his life and teachings strongly affirm the concern of God with the whole of creation. Moreover, the apocalyptic element in his thought is arguably a relatively minor one, disappearing almost entirely in John's Gospel. So I think it is more likely that Jesus was not primarily an apocalyptic prophet. He was primarily a "teacher of righteousness" and a healer, and above all a martyr who gave his life to inaugurate a new community of agapeistic love. That seems to me to be the thrust of many of his parables and sayings.

Apocalypse and the anticipation of the end of time

Apocalyptic elements are present in the Gospels, and the Synoptic Gospels put together, in a slightly haphazard way, a number of sayings into an apocalyptic narrative which can be read in a vindictive, literalist, and myopic way. What that shows, in my view, is how easily Jesus could be misunderstood – even though only in part – even by the Gospel editors. It shows how we must continue to reinterpret the life and teachings of Jesus in each new cultural context – which, of course, the church has done throughout the ages. And it shows how the core teachings of Jesus retain their power to pierce the heart and transform the lives of those who find a decisive revelation of God in his person.

J.D. Crossan argues that apocalyptic thought is foreign to the original teaching of Jesus. He presses even further Jeremias's method of discarding material that, he thinks, arises from the interpretations of the early church and seeking the "original teaching" of Jesus by using the criterion of dissimilarity. The original teaching will be found in what is not part of Jewish or early Christian thought, and what is unique to Jesus.

There can be no question that interpretations from church life after the resurrection have affected the records of Jesus' teachings. But it seems to me unduly restrictive to discard everything in Jesus' teachings that is deeply rooted in Jewish thought, or which looks ahead to events after Jesus' death. In particular, Jesus' remarks about the resurrection of the dead and about a future triumph of God's purposes, which illustrate his participation in Jewish arguments between Pharisees and Sadducees, seem central to his gospel.

Crossan is, I think, correct to emphasize that Jesus is not, as Schweitzer thought, mainly concerned with an imminent end of the world. He is concerned with a present crisis, with what Crossan terms "permanent eschatology".[1] This eschatology does not speak about a termination of the universe, but about the ending of a particular way of being in the world, "an overturning of prior values, closed options, set judgments and established conclusions".[2] God's kingdom comes when God is "present, not as eternity beyond us but as advent within us".[3] Eschatology is concerned, not with future fact, but with present experience, which Jesus' teaching and presence evokes, coming as gift and surprise, reversing our prior expectations, motivating radically new forms of action and evaluation.

All this is well said. But there is a negative side to Crossan's interpretation, which I do not find as convincing. We catch a glimpse of it when he asks, "Is immortality a fundamentally idolatrous conception?" Jesus, he thinks, speaks of three simultaneous modes of the kingdom's presence (past, present, and future, run together in a non-linear way), because there is no other world above and beyond this one. Thus Jesus becomes a Zen-like teacher of spiritual illumination, with few if any objective ontological claims about a reality of God whose eternity completes the human future.

It does seem that here Crossan is fulfilling Tyrell's comment against Harnack that those who look to find the "real" Jesus underneath the mistaken overlay of the Gospels will find the reflection of their own faces. There is nothing wrong with seeking to find in Jesus what one believes to be the highest form of spiritual perception. Such a search is likely to play down any apparent definite predictions of future events, in favour of evoking spiritual perceptions of the mysterious yet transforming advent of God in personal experience. Yet the love of a God who is real and who transcends human temporality seems a central part of Jesus' teaching, as does the hope for eternal life with God.

That will, I think, make a difference to the form of human hope for the future. We will hope for a clearer knowledge of God, for a growth into union with God which will make our lives different from how they can ever be in earthly life, and for a deeper disclosure of the true being of the Christ. In brief, Christian hope will be for an advent of Christ in glory that will be universally accessible.

For these reasons, commentators like E.P. Sanders and Gerd Theissen do not think that beliefs about a "return of Jesus" are wholly inventions of the early church. Those beliefs, they think, are likely to reflect Jesus' own strong concern with the establishment of God's kingdom in or soon after his own lifetime.

On the interpretation I have given, there are elements of truth in both positions. Jesus was interested in the kingdom and in ultimate judgment and redemption. But the kingdom of which he spoke was not of (or from) this world. It was a kingdom of the heart, and of the final participation of the heart in God. Thus he was a teacher of wisdom, but he was a teacher who looked for the final rule of divine wisdom as the fulfilment of cosmic history.

I say this because I think it is likely that, however he interpreted it, Jesus did use the imagery of the apocalyptic writings. But it is also likely that, as a profound spiritual teacher, he did not tie himself to the belief (which turned out to be incorrect) that the world would literally come to an end very soon. Talk of terrors, tribulations, and persecutions are commonplace themes in such writings, but their function is to point up the depravity and alienation of the world, and encourage Christians to remain firm in faith. Patience and hope are the main virtues recommended, with a warning not to place too much confidence in social or political solutions to basic human problems.

It is conceivable that Jesus could have warned his disciples of coming persecution, but these apocalyptic horror stories are too metaphorical and cryptic to be used as timetables for the end of the world. It is ironic that, for some Christians, that is precisely what they became.

The end of history

Christian faith is balanced between pessimism about the political future, and hope for a coming rule of justice and peace. Apocalyptic writings deal with this by foretelling judgment and catastrophe for militaristic and oppressive powers, and peace and happiness for those who put their faith in the mercy of God. The book of Revelation is the outstanding example of this mode of thought in the Bible. But two things are important. One is that such apocalyptic thinking is not the heart of the Christian message, any more than Plato's failed attempt to build an ideal state in Syracuse is the heart of Platonism. The other is that the details of apocalyptic thought must be seen as parts of general fantastic, hyperbolic, and imaginative visions, which it is dangerous and absurd to attempt to interpret in literal detail.

The overall picture is that there is a great battle between good and evil, and that good will triumph and evil will be eliminated. In this battle, a small group are chosen to be the vanguard of a new society of true justice and mercy that will grow to influence the whole world. If Jesus used the imagery of such a picture, there can be little doubt that he was not speaking of a literal and violent battle in which Christians are called to take up weapons and kill people. It is, for him, the meek who will inherit the earth. If the Son of man comes in glory, it will be as the Prince of Peace, not an avenging angel.

Will such a thing happen on this earth? Will it happen soon? No one can know, for it partly depends upon human freedom and responsiveness to divine grace. What matters is that we should be aware that the battle is serious, that it takes place in our own hearts as well as in historical events, and that we are called to be on the side of the peacemakers. Moreover, if we are we will be vindicated, for evil will not finally triumph, however bad things seem to be getting.

So we may pray for the ending of a world of injustice and the horrors of war. But we also pray, at the same time, that new lives may spring up which can enjoy the beauties of the world and realize their unique gifts in new ways. How can we ask for both? This paradox is part of human life. We want good things (like the flourishing of our children) that can only come to be in a world of many evils. We desire the extermination of evil, but not the ending of every finite good. We want, in short, the transfiguration of the world, so that the evil will disappear and the good will shine in even greater detail and beauty. But it is hard to see how that can occur while human wills remain free and continue to choose self and desire over the objective reality of goodness.

We need to see, in the very earliest Christian church, a gradual dawning of the idea that God's purpose is truly universal, not limited to a renewal of the nation state of Judah, and that God's love is truly universal, so that it always aims at healing and human good and not at injury and human harm. The apocalyptic passages in the Gospels and letters tend to look for an end of history before God's universal purpose has been worked out, and they tend to exclude huge numbers of people from the divine love. If the coming of the Son of man literally comes like Noah's flood, it will put an end to any positive purpose for the world and it will destroy the vast majority of human lives.

For this reason, a truly positive gospel will teach that the end of history will not come before God's purpose has been worked out as fully as possible, and that no one is destroyed without the possibility of repentance and new life in God. Nevertheless, it will hold that evil will eventually be removed from creation, that all good things will be conserved, and that evil things will wherever possible be transformed in the life and experience of God.

Parables like that of the great division are primarily exhortations to keep awake to make sure that you do not fall into evil, to persist in goodness, and to trust that God will give you a share in eternal life. They are reminders to you to be vigilant in goodness, not predictions that you may be destroyed, much less threats to others that they will be destroyed (or, even worse, that you are given licence to destroy them).

History will not come to a sudden end with an appearance of Jesus in the clouds at any moment. Given that such beliefs can be found within the New Testament, today we have to ask what gave rise to them, and whether we can appropriate them in any sense. One thing that should be clear is that on any literal interpretation the so-called "second coming" should have happened thousands of years ago, but it did not happen. That puts an end to any hope of finding in the Bible a completely inerrant set of beliefs about the future of the planet earth.

It is possible for Christians today to agree that Jesus did fulfil prophecy, that he was raised from the dead, and that he was the one to establish the rule of God on earth in a new way. But his kingdom is not a political kingdom; it is the rule of God in the heart. That is the decisive key to the reinterpretation of the role of Jesus in world history. History goes on, and the kingdom operates in a hidden way amid the terrors of history. Christians are to work to extend the kingdom, the rule of self-giving love in the world, without expecting its historical success – for human wills remain free and largely estranged from a God of love. Yet it is natural to hope that what can be partly true of the heart may one day be fully true in external reality, as it is now true "in heaven" for those blessed few who are living with God and are now under the rule of the glorified Christ. What Christians can hope for is that when the history of human freedom in this world has come to an end, evil will be abolished and love will be triumphant. The kingdom will be present fully, openly, and universally. Christians must now commit themselves to a self-sacrificial moral goal of seeking justice and universal compassion, to an acceptance of the ambiguity of the world, to a liberating experience of the presence of God in Christ, and to a final hope for the triumph of good.

Is this well represented by parables of Noah's flood and the disappearance of people from their beds in the night? Not if the parables are taken out of context and in isolation, and interpreted literally. The New Testament as a whole would not stress destruction by God, but the self-destructiveness of evil and the emptiness of life without God; not a clear-cut division into good and bad, but the moral ambiguity of all lives and the universal need for grace; not an angry God and the saving of a small elect, but our rejection of a loving God and God's forgiving and transforming love for all.

The great division

Can we imagine the Jesus of the Sermon on the Mount calling down floods and volcanic eruptions on his enemies? Can we imagine him taking to himself a few people, those who are extremely good or who genuinely repent, and leaving the rest to destruction? To me that is unthinkable.

Then we must seek another interpretation of the parables of the great division. Jesus used images drawn from the Hebrew Bible to warn of coming catastrophe for Israel (the flood and the fire), to teach that there is a real division between good and evil (the taking from fields and beds), and to make an urgent call for turning to accept God's love (watching for the coming of the Son of man, who will triumph not in war but in love).

There is judgment and division. But there is also God's unlimited love and the open invitation to turn back to God. Which of these strands of thought is stressed depends largely on context. Jesus'

situation was one in which Jewish rebellion against Rome was almost
inevitable and doomed to disaster. It was one in which the call to
violence had to be resisted, and in which it was imperative to make
a clear and decisive choice. The right choice might require great
personal sacrifice; but it would lead to the victory of love. But that
victory would not finally come until the whole world order had been
decisively changed.

Some of us (only a few) are lucky enough to live in a very different
situation. We live in free and democratic societies that are not subject
to brutal violence and tyranny. New scientific discoveries offer the
hope of an improvement of life for millions of people. There is a
positive hope for the future of the earth. Nevertheless, we still live
with the possibility of the destruction of the earth, whether by nuclear
or biological weapons or by meteorites from space. The world could
easily collapse into anarchy and chaos, and millions still starve and are
violently killed in the most appalling ways.

In that sense, the gospel message is the same for us as it was in Jesus'
time. There is a real battle between good and evil, between serving
love and controlling power. In such a world, we must work for the
good whatever the cost. We must "look for the kingdom", or watch
for the coming of the king, and not give up in despair or apathy. We
may hope and believe that the purposes of God, revealed in Christ,
will be realized, but possibly – even probably, given the facts of human
freedom – that will not be on this earth.

The early hope for a quick end to tragic human history was
transformed by the realization that God has many unfinished
purposes yet for the world, and there may well be future generations
who will have a part in realizing them. This was a realization that only
fully came after the New Testament documents had been compiled.
So our faith has been changing in response to new insights from
the very beginning, while retaining a basic loyalty to the nature and
purposes of God discerned in the person of Jesus. The challenge for
us is to become fully conscious of this and accept it as part of our
understanding of revelation – a growth into truth, guided by the
Spirit of Christ.

These parables belong to times of terror and violence. They counsel patience and hope, and they need to be balanced by the parables of forgiveness and compassion. Taken in isolation and interpreted as predictions of the near future, the parables of the great division may well seem judgmental and morally severe. They should rather be seen as stories which emphasize the necessity of making a decisive commitment to the Spirit of self-giving love, in a world that is lost in self-destructive hatred and ignorance. Yet they remind those of us who live in freedom and luxury that evil is real and stalks the world, and we must make a decisive choice as to where we stand in a world filled with terror and violence, however remote from us it may seem.

Be ready

Keep awake. It is as if the house owner has gone away, leaving you to work and to keep watch. The owner may return suddenly, and find you asleep. Or if you neglect your duties, and beat the other servants and get drunk, he will cast you out. Or perhaps a thief will come, and you will be caught sleeping. Therefore keep awake, work and watch.

This group of parables, found in Mark 13:33–37, Matthew 24:42–51, and Luke 12:39–46, expounds the theme of present responsibility and unexpected return.

As I have argued, the Gospel editors may have thought of this in terms of the imminent return of Christ in glory. Disciples are not to give up work because the present world order is about to come to an end anyway, or because they are dispirited at the seeming absence of the Lord, or because they begin to doubt the possibility of the kingdom's arrival. They are to be diligent in doing good, in seeking justice, and in caring for others, just as if they expected the Lord's return (or the arrival of a thief) at any moment.

Jeremias, in his close analysis of these parables, suggests that it is very odd to think of the return of Christ as a thief. He proposes that Jesus' own teaching was probably a warning of imminent catastrophe. If the people did not turn to a non-violent and compassionate relationship

with God, there would be terrors to come for Israel. That warning was
appropriate, since Israel was in fact destroyed by the Romans, partly
because of the many violent uprisings that messianic pretenders like
Judas of Galilee had instigated. Then, Jeremias proposes, the early
church gave the parable a Christological twist, turning it into a counsel
of patience in view of the delayed return of Christ.[4] That is certainly
possible, though if both judgment and redemption are supra-temporal
realities, then Jesus might well have seen both the destruction of
Jerusalem and the birth of a new covenant community of the Spirit as
historical anticipations of such a supra-temporal and spiritual reality.

We do not know whether Jesus thought that history would end
fairly soon, though we know that some early disciples did. But I think
the important point is that the spiritual meaning remains even when
the expectation of an immediate end has faded. After all, when earthly
time has ended the kingdom will exist in its fullness. Christ will be
fully present and clearly known. Moreover, that end will not just be in
some remote future. Every moment of time will be taken into it and
be either transformed or rejected in that eternal fulfilment of history
when all time is taken into the eternal reality of God.

The old world order of a sacrificial priesthood and a nation centred
on the Temple in Jerusalem did come to an end with the destruction
of the Temple and of the city of Jerusalem. The new world order that
was inaugurated was a spiritual, not a political, order. That is, it was
an order in which the divine Spirit ruled in the hearts of men and
women, not an order in which one nation or institution was divinely
commissioned to rule the world, or in which a perfect society actually
existed on earth.

So we are to seek the Good with all our energy, as if the Lord will
be fully present at any moment. For eternity is not remote and far off.
It is always "near at hand", a goal that is beyond time, and so is equally
near to every time, and yet will not be overtly present until time has
ended. It is the existing ideal of active goodness. We must seek to
realize it (or rather, let it be realized) in our own lives and in the world
as far as is possible, even though it will always in this temporal world be
frustrated by the many misuses of human freedom. Its full realization

is in God, and we shall share in it when God comes to us to take us into the divine eternity.

That resolute pursuit of the Good, and the insight that the Good actively seeks us before we seek it, and will ensure that it is fully realized in the fulfilment of all time (the *telos*, usually translated as "end" of time) is put into the symbols of Hebrew prophetic discourse by saying that we must do the work God gives us as if the Lord whom we serve will return unexpectedly. If we work as we should, that will be an event of great joy. So we need not fear or despair at apparent frustrations and defeats. The Lord will come and take us to himself, and such divine love cannot be defeated. In fact we should eagerly await the return of the Lord – that is to say, we should look forward to the presence of God at every moment, however dark and hopeless it would otherwise seem.

Summary

This group of parables uses the apocalyptic imagery of a "day of wrath", a terrible judgment on the nations of the world, and an imminent return of the Son of man with angels in glory to inaugurate the kingdom of God. Such images belong to a specifically Jewish eschatological typology and need to be revised (as John's Gospel revised them) to provide a broader picture of Christ as cosmic judge and redeemer in a vast cosmos. The fact that the return did not happen in the generation of the disciples shows conclusively that a literal interpretation of these parables is impossible for us. I suggest that a valid and helpful spiritual interpretation is to take the images as pictures of how we stand in relation to God, and of what God wills for our future. We stand "under judgment", in a world condemned to die. But we also stand "under grace", in a world redeemed by the sacrificial love of Christ. The day of wrath and the day of redemption are the same day. There is no judgment without the possibility of redemption; and there is no redemption without the reality of judgment. Each day of our lives is an anticipation, a prolepsis, of our ultimate standing before God. We may not know what we shall be on that day. But we know what God wills us to be, what God makes it possible for us to be, and what God calls us to be. The gospel transforms the apocalyptic imagery of judgment into the gospel imagery of redemption through love, the imagery of the coming of the Son of man in glory to take us to be where he is. We must be aware that our lives continually stand under the judgment of God for their failure to be just, merciful, and benevolent. But we must also be aware of the possibility of redemption through love at every moment.

Part 4

The Ethics of Personal Fulfilment
Parables of the Spirit-Led Life

Many of Jesus' parables do not use imagery about future events on earth. They are rather about what Paul calls the Spirit-led life, and Matthew sees as the life of the kingdom. Thus Matthew speaks of the kingdom primarily as a way of living in the world, a way which Paul sees as inspired by the divine Spirit. For both, that way will find its ultimate fulfilment beyond this world. These parables form the third of the groups I have distinguished. They provide moral teachings of a sort, but not new moral rules or precepts. They teach not what we should do, but how we should be, in the light of the disclosure of the divine love in and through Jesus.

Jesus and the *Torah*

The attitude of Jesus to the statutes and ordinances of the Jewish law, the *Torah* (613 of them, according to tradition), has been much debated. The early nineteenth-century German scholar F.C. Baur expressed a widely held view that Jesus' morality was quite new, and essentially different from Jewish "legalism". Jesus, said Baur, emphasized the inner as opposed to the outer, and the spirit as opposed to the letter of the law. The antitheses of the Sermon on the Mount ("you have heard... but I say to you") can be taken to show a renunciation of traditional religious laws. Mark 7:19 (translated in the Revised Standard Version, for example, as "Thus he declared all foods clean") could point to Jesus' abolition of the Jewish food laws. And his attitudes to healing (Mark 3:1–6) and plucking corn (Mark 2:23–28) on the sabbath, to being touched by a ritually unclean woman (Mark 5:27), and to matters of ritual washing (Mark 7:1–8) have been taken to show that he was rather lax in keeping the religious laws.

More recently, however, E.P. Sanders,[1] Geza Vermes, and others have argued that all Jesus' teachings and actions are well within the range of possible interpretations of Jewish law. After all, just before the antitheses of the Sermon on the Mount, Jesus (according to Matthew) says, "Do not think that I have come to abolish the law or the prophets. I have come not to abolish but to fulfil" (Matthew 5:17). The Markan phrase from Mark 7:19, which Mark himself may well have intended as a declaration of the ritual cleanliness of all foods, is very obscure. In Greek (in one version) it reads: "*katharizon panta ta bromata*", literally, "purifying all foods". Thus it could easily be read as saying that all foods are cleansed from the body when they pass out into the drain. Geza Vermes suggests that the Aramaic original could have read "food passes out into the place where all excrement is purged away".[2] Alternatively, the phrase could be a parenthesis by Mark to give Mark's own much later interpretation of what Jesus' teaching implied. In no case is it a direct declaration by Jesus that the food laws are obsolete, and it seems most unlikely that he could have said such a thing.

As for the sabbath healings, Sanders and others have shown that healing and such things as plucking corn on the sabbath are allowed in some cases of need. In the text, Jesus defends his conduct by appeal to Scripture, which suggests that he is not abolishing the law. He is, however, opposing very conservative interpretations that would limit healing and food preparation on the sabbath to cases where there is a danger of death. So he is acting on a wide and humane interpretation of the law. When Jesus criticizes the Pharisees for their addiction to various ritual practices, he does not say that they should give them up. What he says is that they should attend to "the weightier matters of the law" like justice, mercy, and the love of God, but "without neglecting the others" (Luke 11:42 and Matthew 23:23). There is little justification here for a wholesale rejection of the *Torah*. As Professor Sanders says bluntly, "Jesus did not teach his disciples that they could break either the Sabbath or the food laws."[3]

I have always thought that the decisive factor is that almost all those who had known Jesus personally were in favour of keeping the Jewish law for early Christians. Peter even wondered whether he should associate with Gentiles and only did so after a vision (Acts 10:9–29), not because of anything Jesus had said. This is a very strong indication that Jesus had never explicitly taught that the observance of the *Torah* was unimportant. I conclude that Jesus upheld the *Torah* throughout his teaching. That is no doubt why he does not enunciate a list of new moral principles, as he might have done – something explicit about political obligations, human rights, the equality of men and women, or slavery, might have been welcome. But 613 laws were probably enough, and rabbinic interpretations, extrapolations, and inferences from them provide enough material for any ethicist to work on.

Nevertheless, Jesus did emphasize a distinctive element in his moral teaching. It must be kept in mind that his whole teaching was to Jews. He did not, it seems, want them to renounce the *Torah*, but he did want them to see that the heart of the *Torah* is not slavish obedience to rules given by divine command. It is an expression of loving obedience to God, with the emphasis on the word "loving". We will gladly obey rules if we believe that they are given for our good (Deuteronomy 10:13: "Keep the commandments of the Lord your God... for your own well-being") by a being who is supremely desirable, beautiful, and good ("As a deer longs for flowing streams, so my soul longs for you, O God", Psalm 42:1). If we believe that God is supremely desirable, we will love God. If we love God, we will want to be like God. What Jesus does is to penetrate beyond mere obedience to rules to see how such rules help us to be more like God. For instance, we are to love our enemies because God "is kind to the ungrateful and the wicked". We are to be "merciful, just as your Father is merciful" (Luke 6:35–36). And in Jesus' "new commandment", we are to "love one another as I have loved you" (John 13:34).

We are, in short, to be imitators of God, and Jesus' disciples are to be imitators of God as God is revealed in Jesus' own person. Though Jesus, in his ministry to the Jewish people, taught that the *Torah* should be obeyed, what was important was that this should be the obedience of love. The greatest commandment, Jesus said, is that you should "love the Lord your God" (Mark 12:29). Love is admiration and respect; it is imitation and emulation; and it is, at its highest, participation in and union with the being of the beloved. True obedience to the *Torah* is a personal and social expression of such reverence, imitation, and participation.

After the death of Jesus, the disciples were right in gradually seeing that Gentiles were not bound by circumcision or the Mosaic covenant, but that Jesus, who is the incarnation of the eternal wisdom of God, would become their *Torah*. In his person they could see the pattern of perfected love. When the Gospels were written, it was already apparent that the age of the Temple priesthood had ended and that Jesus' warnings of the end of the nation of Judah had found a terrible fulfilment. Among the largely Gentile people of the new covenant the Mosaic laws as a whole were no longer binding.

In about the third century after Christ, Jewish rabbis formulated the *sheva mitzvot*, seven laws of the children of Noah, obligations for humanity in general. They are: do not blaspheme; do not worship idols; do not murder; do not commit adultery; do not steal; establish courts of justice; and do not eat a limb from a living animal (forbidding cruelty to animals).[4] They are very general principles, but they point to the fact that there are universal moral principles, as well as to the fact that their details are to be worked out in specific circumstances by rational thought. There is no question here of a blind obedience to specific rules laid down by God.

That does not mean that the Jewish law had become wholly irrelevant. According to Matthew, Jesus had said that "until heaven and earth pass away, not one letter, not one stroke of a letter, will pass from the law until all is accomplished" (Matthew 5:18). Some commentators have tried to say that all was accomplished when Jesus rose from death. But since heaven and earth still exist, I do not find that convincing. Some, like Calvin, have suggested that the ritual and hygienic laws are obsolete, but the moral laws remain in force. But it is not easy to say precisely which laws are moral and which are ritual – for example, is "Keep the sabbath day" moral or ritual? In any case, it is completely foreign to the Jewish understanding of the *Torah* to make that sort of distinction. All the laws are given by God, and though there are many weighty issues of interpretation to be settled, no orthodox Jew would separate out a class of "moral" laws and say that they remain binding while the others can be neglected.

The law remains in force for religious Jews. But for Gentile disciples of Jesus, its precise prescriptive details are not binding. What Gentiles need to do is to discover the deeper general principles that underlie specific laws and work out how to apply them in diverse situations. It is very important for an understanding of Christian morality to note that the early church was left to come to its own decisions about specific moral laws. The disciples had to decide whether the law was to be retained or how much of it was to be retained. They had no specific commands of Jesus to which they could appeal. They had to work out, through discussion and argument (recorded in Acts 15:1–21), what specific moral laws were to be regarded as binding on disciples. And it is important to note that they argued among themselves (it was not just a matter of blind obedience), and that their decisions changed over time (they were not unrevisable). The rule they agreed at the Council recorded in Acts 15 – that Christians should only eat *kosher* or ritually killed meat – was soon rescinded, and modern Christians pay no attention to any religiously prescribed food laws.

The virtues of the Christian life

The general principles that are emphasized more than any others in Jesus' recorded teaching are pretty clear. They are: humility, non-vindictiveness, non-possessiveness, and unlimited generosity. They all follow directly from the basic principle of loving and imitating God. But God is seen in quite a distinctive way by Jesus.

Jesus repeatedly stresses the virtue of humility, and it is well summed up by the phrase "whoever wishes to become great among you must be your servant" (Mark 10:43). Humility is easily mocked as a grovelling subservience which undermines all self-respect. As Aristotle said, when writing about the virtues, it is hard to find the middle way between possible extremes. Humility must lie between the extremes of arrogant pride and servile self-deprecation.

Christian humility must be seen primarily as the proper human relationship to God. Perhaps Friedrich Schleiermacher captured the idea rather well when he spoke of the Christian life as one that cultivates "the immediate feeling of absolute dependence".[5] Humans are never wholly "self-made" beings, for all that we are and have is absolutely dependent upon God, the ultimate source of all being. God, for Christians, is one who, in Jesus, shares in the suffering of the human condition in order to liberate humanity from sin and estrangement, precisely by facing up to pain and death and showing that they can be overcome by the power of love. God is not weak, for in God is the unconquerable power of eternal life. But God freely takes the role of a servant in order to accomplish an immensely worthwhile goal.

Those who imitate God do not aim at things that satisfy the selfish ego. They aim at the good of others and of the world, and they do so by serving, helping, healing, and teaching – as Jesus did. There are many ways of serving. A king can serve his people by ruling well, and an executive can serve by taking bold executive decisions. Humility does not mean always deferring to others. It means not seeking personal aggrandisement and not seeking the praise of others for its own sake. It also means putting oneself in a position to do the most good, and using gifts and abilities to their fullest extent in the service of others. Humility is a virtue that stands between pride and self-contempt. It gives gratitude to God for all good gifts and works as effectively as possible to promote good and restrain evil.

A second great virtue that resounds throughout Jesus' teaching is mercy. Again and again he teaches the value of forgiveness and non-vindictiveness. We should forgive, he said to Peter, "not seven times, but, I tell you, seventy seven times" (Matthew 18:22), and the Lord's Prayer asks that God should forgive us "as we forgive others". The law allows us to require "an eye for an eye and a tooth for a tooth", but Jesus counsels us not to resist evildoers, but to "turn the other cheek" (Matthew 5:38–41).

It would be absurd to take these remarks as literal rules. We should not refuse to forgive on the seventy-eighth occasion. We should not expect God to forgive us exactly to the extent, no more or less, than we forgive others. And it would be irresponsible if we never resisted evildoers, but allowed them to do whatever they wanted. The point is that we should imitate God, who offers forgiveness to the wicked and does not insist on some exact punishment for every sin. The story in John's Gospel of the woman taken in adultery, whom Jesus forgave (John 8:1–11), ends with his admonition: "Go your way, and from now on do not sin again." God always offers us the chance of repentance and reformation, and will accept sincere efforts to make amends, however inadequate. But even free and full forgiveness requires repentance and preparedness to make a new start. And the fact that God is merciful does not negate the reality of divine judgment on those who remain committed to egoism and injustice.

Mercy is a virtue that stands between vindictiveness and indifference. It imitates the divine offer of unlimited forgiveness, conditional on a resolution to make amends and start again. Jesus' exhortations not to resist evildoers and never to judge others cannot be taken as moral rules. If they were, there would be no Christian police and judges. Yet they have moral force. They place before us, in exaggerated, hyperbolic form, the ideal attitude of non-vindictiveness and compassionate understanding that should qualify our relationships with others in society.

A third major virtue in the moral teaching of Jesus is non-possessiveness. "You cannot serve God and wealth" (Matthew 6:24), Matthew reports. Luke, with his distinctive stress on a gospel for the poor, goes even further: "Sell your possessions and give alms" (Luke 12:33). If this is to be an imitation of the nature of God, it cannot mean that we are literally to possess nothing, to be without even the means of bare subsistence. For God possesses all things and has the power to create rare and beautiful things without limit. We may, however, speak of the poverty of God if we think of the boundless generosity of God, who does not selfishly enjoy the good things of creation, but shares them with others.

Spiritual poverty is not possessing nothing. It is regarding all good things, not as owned by us, but as loaned by God to be used by us for the good of all. To worship wealth is to be primarily concerned about our own pleasure and satisfaction. To worship God is to be primarily concerned about the flourishing of goodness in all creation and the appreciation of that goodness by all God's creatures.

Non-possessiveness is a virtue that stands between egoism and irresponsibility. Humans are stewards of the gifts of God, and those gifts must be used responsibly – not simply for one's own pleasure but for the common good. In this case, too, it would be silly to take Jesus' sayings as precise rules. They commend an attitude of equanimity and dispassion about worldly wealth. We should not be anxious about food or clothing, and we should not try to become wealthy for its own sake. But it is right to be able to give good things in a just and generous manner, and so responsible stewardship, not indiscriminate profligacy, is the virtue of non-possessiveness.

A fourth virtue that plays a major role in Jesus' teaching is the virtue of unlimited generosity. "Give to everyone who begs from you, and do not refuse anyone who wants to borrow from you" (Matthew 5:42). That might be difficult enough, but Jesus goes on to say, "Love your enemies" (Matthew 5:44). Generosity is not to be confined to those whom we like or are indifferent to. It must extend to those whom we dislike, and who seek to oppose or even to destroy us.

What love could mean in such circumstances is very difficult to say. It certainly cannot include a desire to hurt or destroy, and it seems to imply some sort of attempt to procure the well-being of our enemies. Yet it cannot mean that we are to give murderers and rapists whatever they ask for. Albert Schweitzer seems to think that it does mean precisely that, but then he regards this teaching as an "interim ethic" for a short period before the end of history, and for a small socially inferior minority, so it does not have to be realistic.

If you tried to take the moral teachings of Jesus literally you would, however, reach some very odd conclusions, even for an interim ethic. You would, for instance, come to the conclusion that you should hate your father and mother (Luke 14:26) but love your enemies. I think, therefore, that we are forced to see such statements as picturesque, memorable but extreme literary devices for shocking his hearers into reappraising their attitudes to giving and to the treatment of enemies. We should not regard giving as an optional donation of our excess to others, and we should not regard enemies as people to be personally hated.

Many of us would, however, disobey the command, "do not resist evildoers" (Matthew 5:39), taken in a literal sense. If we give it a non-literal interpretation, it could mean that we should not insist on our legal rights, or that, while seeking to restrain evildoers, we should not bar the possibility of bringing them around to a better point of view.

There are no precise instructions here, and it will be up to us to decide how the statement applies in our situation. It is not a matter of a duty which could be enforced by anyone. It is more like an ideal that will have different sorts of application in different circumstances. Its function is to be a background commitment to seeing the best in people and to benevolence, to prevent us from being vindictive and vengeful, without laying down what exactly we ought to do.

This conclusion is reinforced by the fact that the Sermon on the Mount enunciates the so-called "Golden Rule": "Do to others as you would have them do to you" (Matthew 7:12). It is well known by moral philosophers that this is a silly rule if taken literally. For example, it would be silly to treat murderers as you would like to be treated if you were a murderer, since you would probably like to be released and sent on holiday. The Golden Rule has a valuable moral function in reminding us seriously to consider the welfare of others. It is not a substantive moral rule, but a memorable methodological principle, the application of which requires hard moral thinking in specific situations.

This does not mean that there are no moral duties, but it does mean that Jesus does not in general issue new specific moral duties, or even specific interpretations of the duties outlined in the *Torah*. He cites six standard moral commandments when speaking to a rich young man (Matthew 19:16–19), but provides no interpretation of them. When he does appear to interpret the commandments, it is in order to recommend the sort of moral ideals just outlined. Thus when he comments on the commandment not to kill (more exactly, not to "kill unlawfully"), he prohibits anger (without cause, Matthew typically adds), insults, and contempt (Matthew 5:21–22). He does not, as a scholar of the *Torah* might do, specify the exact conditions under which killing might be lawful, but commends general mental attitudes that form part of the background beliefs that should operate when we form our personal moral judgments.

Jesus' moral teaching, then, is a participative virtue ethics. It founds the basic moral attitudes of humility, mercy, non-possessiveness, and unlimited benevolence on reverence for, imitation of, and participation in the character of God as it is revealed in Jesus. It should not be thought that the Gospels set out to give a comprehensive moral theology. They presuppose a humane interpretation of the *Torah*, as well all the rabbinic debates about the *Torah* which are central to Jewish tradition. Seeing morality as imitation of the perfections of God, they presuppose the human commitment to creative activity, to wisdom and understanding, and to enjoyment and appreciation of all good things that follows from the prophetic perceptions of God as a wise creator who delights in the works of creation. They assume that the gospel of Jesus brings light, life, and joy into human lives, as John's Gospel repeatedly stresses.

Why, then, do the Synoptic Gospels emphasize most the virtues of humility, mercy, non-possessiveness, and benevolence? For me, a basic clue lies in Jesus' disputes with the scribes and Pharisees, and in his concern to reform religious life. Jesus is countering a set of vices which are widespread in society, but which unfortunately can be especially strong among religious believers. Pride in being chosen by God, in possessing high status within a religious organization, and in having unique access to truth or salvation is widespread in all forms of religious life. The virtue of humility follows from the fact that Christ, "though he was in the form of God, did not regard equality with God as something to be exploited, but emptied himself, taking the form of a slave" (Philippians 2:6–7). Whether this refers to the pre-existent Christ or to the human Jesus, it certainly commends *kenosis*, self-emptying, as a human excellence. And since human excellences reflect the perfections of God, it expresses the humility of God in setting aside divine glory in the incarnation to share in the limitations of human existence. There is therefore no place for personal pride in the life of a society that seeks to reflect the nature of God revealed in Christ Jesus.

Censoriousness and a tendency to be judgmental of others are also common among religious believers. The virtue of mercy reflects the forgiving and reconciling nature of God as expressed in Jesus. Greed, seen in attempts to gain power and prestige, to control social life and amass property, is common in religion. The virtue of non-possessiveness is a reminder that God gives all good things freely to others, and that the search for wealth and power is not the way of the disciples of Jesus. Intolerance of others, also a common religious vice, is countered by the virtue of unlimited generosity, reminding us that God is kind even to the wicked, and that believers should be distinguished not by hating or seeking to repress their enemies, or those who disagree with them in matters of religion, but by loving them in whatever ways seem appropriate.

The virtues that Jesus stresses are proclaimed in opposition to the characteristic vices of both the political and religious authorities of his day. These sayings were probably selected by the Gospel editors because they were especially relevant to countering some characteristic vices of the early Christian churches with which they were directly concerned. They continue to form a radical critique both of political authorities and of the Christian churches throughout history. The teaching of Jesus has immense moral force, but that force does not consist in the provision of new moral rules. What it consists in can be seen by consideration of what I have called the parables of the Spirit-led life.

The judgment

As you forgive, so you will be forgiven. As you condemn, so you will be condemned. This is the true law of spiritual retribution. (Matthew 6:14–15)

Those who feed the hungry, welcome strangers, clothe the needy, visit the sick and those in prison inherit the kingdom. Those who ignore the hungry, needy, strangers, sick, and imprisoned inherit eternal fire. (Matthew 25:31–46)

Throughout our lives we make ourselves into people who are either judgmental and critical of others or merciful and forgiving to others. The judgment is not a specific future time when a strict sentence is imposed by an external judge. The judgment is what we make of our own lives, when they are fully exposed for what they are, without concealment and when we no longer have the power to impose our will by force.

A "law of spiritual retribution" recurs frequently in the recorded teachings of Jesus. "The measure you give will be the measure you get" (Mark 4:24); "those who are ashamed of me... of them the Son of man will also be ashamed" (Mark 8:38); and "give the money to the poor and you will have treasure in heaven" (Mark 10:21) are typical examples. Such principles are not to be taken as precise predictions for specific cases – as though we will get back exactly what we give, to exactly the same extent. We may well not want what we give to others! The principles teach that what we habitually do to others will shape our most basic character. If we are generous and compassionate, we will become persons who are open to others, and who care about what they think and feel. If we are mean and harsh, our hearts will gradually be closed against the needs of others. Over time, we will become either persons who find happiness in the companionship of kind and caring people, or persons who relate only to others who are also mean and harsh. We will gravitate towards the sort of society that contains others like us. This will be either Paradise or hell, for those who learn love will flourish in a loving society and those who practise self-centredness will wither in a society of ruthless egoists.

This happens partly in earthly life. But it is after earthly life that the full consequences of what we make ourselves become fully apparent. Thus Jesus reveals what we are becoming through our innermost choices and actions, and points out the final destiny towards which those choices are leading us. That is judgment.

The picture language of Matthew 25:31–46 is not to be taken literally. The picture of the glorious throne, the sheep and goats, the kingdom and the eternal fire – all these vividly make the point that there will be a time beyond earthly time when what we have made of our lives will become unequivocally clear. It is a remarkable fact that there is no mention of faith in these passages. All depends upon whether we care for others in practical action, in feeding the hungry, welcoming strangers, clothing the naked, and visiting the sick and imprisoned, or not. Indeed, the goats believe there is a God, but they do not do the works of God. That is what counts. "Faith by itself, if it has no works, is dead" (James 2:17).

Because "all nations" are brought before the throne, it seems to follow that those who are merciful and benevolent, and who show genuine love of others, will inherit the kingdom, even if they did not recognize the presence of God. They do the works of God, and so they are loved by God, and will come to know that the goodness they have revered in action actually exists at the heart of being, and will be revered by them in perfect beauty.

The unstated corollary of these passages is that God is not strict and censorious, but merciful and forgiving. Thus what God requires is not, after all, moral perfection, but regret ("mourning") for our failures and total dependence upon God to help us to do what is right.

To depend wholly on God is to allow divine mercy and love to be realized through us. To be unforgiving is to harden our hearts against the needs of others and against the love of God, which seeks to work in and through us. As we cease to love others and care for their well-being, so we cease to love God – for we cannot love God and be indifferent to those whom God loves ("Whoever does not love does not know God, for God is love", 1 John 4:8). When we cannot love God, we cut our lives off from the source of life and joy. We are imprisoned in our egoistic and self-destructive desires, tortured by our own solitude and hardness of heart (Matthew 18:28–35).

The fact that we think of ourselves as just and righteous only makes our condition worse. A sense of grievance and the veil of self-deceit add to our bitterness and resentment. So we condemn ourselves to a life of misery, recrimination, and despair. That is not what God does to us. It is what we do to ourselves. Yet God's love will never cease. It draws near to us in our darkness, and calls us to respond. That is what it means to say that "the kingdom of heaven has drawn near".

The use of money

The steward who forgives debts is commended because he thereby makes friends for himself if he should be in need. So we should use money to procure for ourselves friendship in heaven. You can use money; but you cannot serve both money and God.

This rather mysterious parable (Luke 16:1–13) speaks of the remission of debts. It could possibly refer to a steward, who is about to be dismissed, cancelling the charging of interest on loans. It certainly speaks of securing future benefits for oneself by a remission of the debts of others. Jesus implies either that forgiving others may procure forgiveness for oneself in heaven ("if you forgive others their trespasses, your heavenly Father will also forgive you", Matthew 6:14), or, on a slightly more literal interpretation, that we should use money to help the poor and needy, so that they may plead for us in heaven.

To this parable are added vaguely related comments – that honesty in small things is important. Honesty in using money, which we have only on trust from God and which is not part of our inner being, is necessary if we are to find our true selves in the kingdom, where there is real spiritual wealth. We must make a choice between seeking wealth and serving God. Money is not evil in itself, but it must be used to do God's will, especially to help those in need. The pursuit of wealth is not of intrinsic value, but must always be instrumental in seeking the welfare of others.

It is not so much that if we do good to others we will get a future reward in heaven. Rather, if we are merciful and benevolent, we make ourselves fit to be members of a society characterized by mercy and benevolence, and only in such a society (the kingdom of heaven) can our true humanity and happiness be fully realized.

The foolishness of riches

A rich man pulled down his barns to build bigger ones, to store his crops and enable him to take his ease, eat, drink, and be merry. But that night he died. A human life does not consist in the abundance of possessions, but in the love of God. You cannot serve God and money.

This parable (Luke 12:13–21) states a recurring theme in Jesus' teaching. We should seek the kingdom of God and not great possessions. Jesus calls at least some of his followers to sell their possessions, give to the poor, and seek an "unfailing treasure in heaven" (Luke 12:33), where there is a society of justice, compassion, and mutual love, rejoicing in the presence of God, whose goodness cannot be destroyed.

This teaching does not call for long-term prudence, saying just that earthly treasure corrupts, while heavenly treasure does not. It calls for a reversal of priorities, from seeking selfish gain and pleasure to seeking what God requires, what is objectively right and good. It is true, however, that "God's service is perfect freedom". Seeking to obey God leads one to love God and to accept God's love, which brings human lives to their proper fulfilment in a conscious relationship to God that can never be overcome. This is a "reward", indeed an eternal reward. But it is a reward that only those who have first become truly good and loving are able to appreciate.

We cannot obtain that reward by our own efforts alone. Only God can give it. What we can do is to turn from the pursuit of self and all the anxieties and frustrations that brings, and place ourselves in the hands of God, to be at God's disposal. Then riches may come to us ("these things will be given to you as well", Luke 12:31). But we will see ourselves as responsible stewards of what belongs to God, not as owners who can do whatever we like with what belongs to us. If wealth or fame or power is what we treasure above all else, it will inevitably be lost. If God is what we treasure above all else, then our hearts will be forever with God.

The unmerciful servant

There was a king who forgave his servant an enormous debt out of pity when the servant pleaded for patience and promised to try and pay the debt. But that servant would not forgive the much smaller debts that others owed to him. So the king put the unmerciful servant in prison until all his debt was paid. So God will do to you if you do not forgive your brother from your heart.

This passage (Matthew 18:21–35) implies that our debts to God (named as much more than fifteen years' wages) cannot ever be fully paid. Not only do we continually fail in love, justice, and mercy; we are not able to love God as we should and we fail to consider the needs of others. We need to be "made anew", or reborn ("No one can see the kingdom of God without being born from above", John 3:3) and to have our old egoistic selves set aside.

It is the Spirit of God, which is brought near to us in the person of Jesus, that renews us. To receive the Spirit we need four things: genuine sorrow for sin, a resolution to make amends as far as we can, preparedness to accept penitential discipline where we cannot make amends, and total dependence upon the mercy and love of God. Where these things exist, the Spirit will work in us what we cannot, and reconcile us to God despite our own inabilities and imperfections.

But to receive God's forgiveness we need to forgive others their sins against us. And we need to do so without limit ("seventy times seven", Matthew 18:22). This does not mean that we should just overlook the wrongdoing of others. Penitence, contrition, and a true change of heart are preconditions of forgiveness and reconciliation. But it does mean that vindictiveness and the desire for vengeance are completely ruled out. It means that we should never hate others, but should take the initiative in opening the door to reconciliation. We should always be concerned about the long-term welfare of those who have wronged us, and never simply wish for their destruction. And we should be merciful in small things, as God has been merciful to us in great things.

It may be thought that the unmerciful servant would remain in prison forever, since he could never repay such a huge debt. But a simple way of release always remains. When the servant learns truly to forgive and learns what real contrition is, then God himself is bound by his own law to forgive without limit. What the servant cannot pay, God will pay. The door to reconciliation is never closed.

Lazarus and the rich man

The rich, who ignore the poor at their gates, are in danger of Hades. Lazarus, the poor man, goes to "Abraham's bosom", and there is a great gulf between them.

This parable (Luke 16:19–31) continues the theme that indifference to the poor and needy leads to torment. While it cannot be taken literally (Abraham's bosom is not big enough for all the poor of the world to rest on), this parable implies an additional dimension to the picture of the kingdom. As well as the kingdom of the heart, the kingdom on earth, and the final kingdom of heaven at the consummation of all things, there is an intermediate state. There the dead exist, either in Hades (*Sheol* – the world of the dead) or in Paradise ("Abraham's bosom").

In Hades there is the torment of fire. In Paradise there is comfort and the companionship of the saints. It is noteworthy that Abraham is there (as are Moses and Elijah at the transfiguration of Jesus). Jesus promises the penitent thief that they will be together in Paradise (Luke 23:43), while Jesus also descends to Hades after his death (1 Peter 3:18–19), before ascending to glory in heaven (1 Peter 3:22).

Thus Paradise is not reserved only for Christians, for those who have known Jesus. Lazarus himself, of course, was not a Christian, but is simply described as a poor man – though presumably he was also good. Nevertheless, Paradise is one meaning of the kingdom of heaven, since in it Jesus now rules as king in glory, "at the right hand of the Father". The implication is that there are new experiences in Paradise, both companionship with the saints and a new realization that Christ, whom one may never have known or even heard of on earth, reigns as king.

There is a gulf fixed between *Sheol* and Paradise. But there is no implication that the gulf will remain forever. In most Jewish thought, after due time, there is release from *Sheol*. If God desires that all should know and love God, and if new experiences are possible in the intermediate state, then it would seem that penitence and release are possible. Perhaps there is even a hint in the parable that the rich man begins to ask for mercy, and to have compassion on his brothers.

The parable of the prodigal son suggests that, when penitence is genuine and the man "comes to his senses" and desires to make amends, God will accept him with joy that one who was dead can now live. If this is so, then this parable retains all the severity of the moral command to help the poor, and yet it is good news indeed of God's invincible love for the whole world.

The workers in the vineyard

Many work long and hard in the vineyard, and they receive what they were promised. But some work only for an hour, and they are paid the same. Those who worked the day long may grumble at this. But even those who enter the kingdom

in the last hour receive the fullness of the love of God. And those who seem to have
done most will not precede those who may seem to have done little and late.

This parable, from Matthew 20:1–16, suggests that God does not judge
as humans judge, for God sees the secrets of the heart, not success in
terms of observable behaviour and the achieving of observable results.
So it may be that the pious who obey the moral law and who work hard
for justice receive less than those who rely wholly and simply on God's
mercy (the message of the parable of the Pharisee and the publican, Luke
18:9–14). For the former may resent not being especially rewarded for
their virtue and diligence, while the latter make no claims upon God.
It is in this sense that "the last [those who are not among the great
and the good of the world] will be first, and the first [those who insist
upon a due reward for their efforts] last" (Matthew 20:16).

Sometimes Christians who have worked hard in the cause of God
think that they deserve more than others, or ask why it is worth working
for God if everyone will receive God's mercy anyway in the end. Thereby
they reveal a certain secret hardness of heart and their lack of real love
for others. If they truly love others, they will desire for them the joy
of knowing God, without requiring some sort of examination in moral
success. And they will themselves work for God out of joy of the divine
presence and gratitude for divine grace.

It is wise not to insist upon a moral examination of one's own life,
for there is a real risk of failure. All are brought near to God by God's
mercy alone. Yet having received that mercy, we will pursue justice, not
in response to the stern voice of duty, but in response to the divine
love. That love takes three forms: first, the love of God for us, despite
all our failures and deceits; second, our grateful love for the God who
has mercy upon us; and third, the love of God within the human heart,
by which we are united intimately with God by the power of God's love
itself. Those who seem to have little in this world may be truly rich,
because they are filled with the power of a love that cannot diminish
or be destroyed.

The use of God's gifts

Human beings have various kinds and degrees of ability, given to them by God. We can use these gifts in ways that increase the material, moral, and spiritual wealth of the world. Or we can let them remain unused. If we do not use our gifts, they will be taken from us, and we will be left in the solitude of our own anxiety and fear.

This parable occurs in slightly different forms in Matthew 25:14–30 and Luke 19:11–27. In both cases, it concludes with one of those highly counter-intuitive sayings that are so typical of Jesus: "to every one who has will more be given; but from him who has not, even what he has will be taken away". This obviously cannot mean that God will give the rich even more money and deprive the poor of what they have. That would contradict the clear teaching of the Gospels that the rich will be sent empty away and the poor will be raised up. In context, it is those who use their gifts well and fruitfully who will achieve joy and fulfilment. Those who bury their gifts, whether out of fear of failure or lack of effort and application, will lose all that they have. They have failed in the task that life set before them, they have failed to realize the potential that God gave, and thus they have rejected the life that was theirs to use but not to possess for themselves.

The deepest message of the parable is that nothing we possess is truly possessed by us. Everything belongs to God, and what we have is given to us in trust and on loan ("The land shall not be sold in perpetuity, for the land is mine; with me you are but aliens and tenants", Leviticus 25:23). As such, all things must be used in the service of God in order to realize justice and mercy and to actualize the good possibilities that are inherent in creation.

According to the first Genesis story of creation, when God created humans he gave them "dominion" over all living creatures on earth, and said to them, "Fill the earth and subdue it" (Genesis 1:28). In the second Genesis story of creation, God put Adam in the Garden of Eden "to till it and keep it" (Genesis 2:15). The Hebrew word for "dominion" is *radah*, which means to rule over, or even to tread down, and the word for "subdue" is *kadash*, which means to keep under control.

Some have argued that these phrases give humans an improper dominance and importance on earth, and even that they are responsible for the modern destructive misuse of the earth's resources. However, the Genesis stories clearly state that God created the earth and the creatures on it and saw that they were good. God loves them and cares for them and enjoys their existence. So it must be wrong to destroy things irresponsibly. Indeed, we must care for the earth as part of our responsibility to "till and keep it". And we must revere the creatures of the earth precisely because they belong to God, who cherishes them for themselves.

As part of our responsibility, we must tread down those things that threaten the well-being of the environment. We must prevent viruses from destroying human life, tigers from eating human beings, and (insofar as we can) cultivate the ground and domesticate animals to provide a secure and productive environment. Humans have real responsibility, but belief in creation should lead us to cherish the earth and its creatures, and act responsibly so that many good things may come into being and flourish. That is precisely what the productive use of God's gifts to us consists in.

Luke prefaces this parable by saying that it was told because "they supposed that the kingdom of God was to appear immediately" (Luke 19:11). Such a belief could lead to an irresponsible attitude that we need not care about the earth because God will renew it quite soon. The parable reminds us that the kingdom is also something that grows, that acts like yeast in bread, that calls us to work creatively in order to bring into being the good things that are inherent in our time-bound world.

There are two major ethical issues in the world today, and they are closely connected. One is how to avoid the danger posed to the environment by modern industrial activity. The other is how to achieve a reasonably just world order, in which all humans have access to food, water, health care, and housing, and freedom from violence and oppression. Moreover, all sentient life, created as good by God, must be cherished, insofar as that is possible in a world in which there are bound to be conflicts of interest, where humans must exercise responsible dominion. There are no easy political answers. But there is no doubt that part of the world's population has more than enough, while most people in the world have not enough to eat.

It is a basic Christian responsibility to try to ensure that the environment God has created is preserved and honoured, so that the beauty of the earth will manifest the glory of God. It is part of the same responsibility to strive for a society in which all the people God has created, without exception, have the opportunity to realize the unique gifts with which God has endowed them.

This means that Christians cannot ignore the environment and the needs of God's creatures. It means that there is a positive purpose in the existence of the world, which is the realization of the many diverse forms of beauty and goodness that the world makes possible. It means that those who look simply for an early end to the present world order have not yet seen the fullness of the purposes that God has in store for the world. We may, and as Christians we must, look for the fullness of all things in God (the "end", the *telos*, the completed purpose of all things). But the history of the cosmos which will contribute to that fullness must continue until all creative possibilities for good have been sufficiently realized. We cannot tell when that will be.

We are not simply to reject the world and leave it to its own devices, having our eyes only on a heaven that lies beyond our world. We are to work in the world to bring it to realize more fully the good things for the sake of which God created it. Creation has a purpose and goal, and humans have a part to play in achieving it. The kingdom may never come fully on earth. But we have a vocation to realize as much of it as is possible in an estranged and disordered world. It is that vocation, and the long story of human failures and successes in attempting to realize it, to which this parable points.

On love of neighbour

We are to love our neighbours "as ourselves". But our neighbours are to include those who disagree with us on fundamental matters of faith, morality, and politics, and those who are enemies of our family or country. Religious and moral beliefs can be causes of hostility to those who differ from us. Love, however, will always take care of the needs of others, whatever their beliefs and behaviour, and have regard for

their health and welfare. "Love of neighbour" is not only love of those who are near
and dear to us. It is dispassionate concern for all life. It is universal love.

We are not to put concern for our own happiness first, but we are to have
concern for the happiness of others, without restriction of family, tribe, or nation.

The parable of the "good Samaritan" (Luke 10:29–37) offers a view
of love so extreme that no one can possibly live up to it. In fact, like
the "Golden Rule" (Matthew 7:12), of which it is one formulation,
it cannot possibly be taken literally. It is not possible to have as great
a concern for everyone on earth as for ourselves. At most we could
manage such concern for a few people, usually those with whom we are
in personal contact.

Therefore this is more of a general guideline for life than a moral
rule. It directs us to extend our moral concern as widely as possible,
and never directly to intend the harm of others, whatever their
beliefs or social position. While it is not a specific moral rule, this
instruction has penetrating force. It implies that we should consider
all people as objects of moral concern, not discriminating on grounds
of gender, class, intelligence, or race, for example. It implies that we
should not disregard the needs and concerns of anyone. It implies
that we should not act at the expense of others, or in ways that cause
them avoidable harm.

Love implies respect for personal autonomy, appreciation of the
unique qualities of others, compassion for the needs of others, and co-
operation with the morally acceptable projects and goals of others. Our
"neighbours" are likely to be those we come into personal contact with,
or those for whom we have a special responsibility. But we should seek
to extend the range of our concern as widely as possible. Compassion
and co-operation must be exercised with care and discrimination, and
this calls for much wisdom and practical judgment. Love without
wisdom can be irresponsible, but wisdom without love can be callous.

We need to work out with wisdom what such love means in our
own situation. And we need to work out how to balance such universal
concern with the claims of family and friends, and indeed with the
obligation to nurture the unique personal gifts we have (Luke 19:12–

27).

Love of neighbour does not depend upon belief in God. In some cases belief in God might wrongly lead us to disregard or mistreat others. Yet the first "great" commandment, love of God, forbids hatred of anything God has made, and enjoins reverence and concern for the proper flourishing of all that God has made, except insofar as something frustrates the purposes of God.

The principle of neighbour love reminds us that God desires the welfare and flourishing of every human person without exception. The commandment to love God gives an overwhelmingly powerful reason for pursuing concern for all human persons. This is not out of fear of punishment, but out of pure love for God, who is supreme beauty and perfection, and whose creativity and awareness is dimly reflected in every human life. These two commandments together define the life of the one who loves the Good in itself and in all its manifestations, and whose life is, insofar as any human life can be, supremely happy.

The far country

The kingdom of heaven is not just for the morally perfect. It is for those who have failed or done wrong and who repent and come to God in submission and with desire to serve faithfully. But the king does not simply wait for submission. He goes out to seek those who are lost and rejoices when they return. So the Teacher seeks especially those who are poor, weak, or socially unacceptable, to seat them at his table.

Those who serve God faithfully and obey his laws must not insist upon their merits and their worthiness, or resent God's love for the penitent. They should rejoice with their king that what was lost is found again. So the severity of the demands of the kingdom is mitigated, and penitence and faithful love are accepted in place of moral perfection. The righteous also may need penitence for their complacency and misplaced sense of moral superiority.

The parable of the prodigal son (Luke 15:11–32) stands in contrast to the stringent demands of the Sermon on the Mount and Matthew's harsh division between the righteous and the wicked in the parable of the cornfield. Stringent moral demands remain in force; but moral failure is embraced and transformed by love – the active, seeking, healing love of

God and the responsive, grateful, penitent love of men and women.

The parable presents a picture of the nature of human life and its source and goal in God. There is that which is supremely good and beautiful, from which all finite things flow as finite images of its changeless eternity. This, the being of God, expresses itself by the necessity of love, and from it every finite form unfolds. But the world is not and never was wholly good. It exists to engender forms of goodness that are essentially diverse, developing, and difficult to achieve. Our world is a self-organizing, growing, and creatively diverse whole that generates organic life forms of intelligence and freedom. They need to be brought gradually into being through a long process that involves struggle and conflict, failure as well as success. This world contains endeavour and tragedy, but in it forms of goodness exist which otherwise could not be. Those forms of goodness can be completed and fully realized in the life of eternity, and only then can their necessity and meaning be fully perceived.

In this world, between the primordial perfection of pure Goodness and the final perfection of a communion of love, there lies the possibility of estrangement and alienation, as finite persons, formed of dust and desire, pursue their own self-centred interests and short-sighted goals. So it is that we take the gifts of life and possibility, and spend them to gain power, wealth, and fame. So it is that we journey into a far country, and, spending and getting, waste all that we have and are. In that place of estrangement God comes to meet us, to raise us, with evil purged and goodness transfigured, to the feast of eternal joy. Thus the good purpose of creation is achieved, and love is attained through the overcoming of selfish desire.

But there is an unexpected twist to this story. Love is not achieved by strenuous effort, and selfish desire is not overcome by discipline alone. It is when we admit our inadequacy that the active love of God meets and embraces us. The power that overcomes selfish desire is not our own but the power of divine love, which we receive in the knowledge that it is wholly undeserved.

The "elder son" of the parable represents those who obey what they perceive to be the commandments, and who serve God faithfully, as they see it. Yet they are jealous of their privileges, conscious of their faithful service, and angry at those who have been less faithful and obedient. In Matthew's parable of the cornfield, God throws the evil into the fire, and takes the good to himself. But in Luke's parable of the prodigal son, it is the good who refuse to share in the feast of the kingdom, and the evil who, repentant and surprised, are taken into the kingdom with joy.

Luke's Jesus said, "I have come to call not the righteous but sinners to repentance" (Luke 5:32). The people whom Jesus criticizes are the religious and the pious (Luke 11:37 – 12:1). He accuses them of being concerned with the correct observance of rituals, of pride in the observance of religious laws, of love of honour and dignity. Yet they do not really care for justice, mercy, and the inner love of God. It is not that observance of religious and moral law is bad. Sincere goodness is acceptable to God. Yet those who take pride in their goodness, who put the observance of laws above the demands of common human need, and who wish their respectability to be honoured by others, make themselves unable to share the kingdom with the penitent poor.

Two things follow from these parables, taken together. First, what is required is true goodness, the love of others from the heart, whatever their social or moral failings, and the subordination of social and conventional respectability to real concern with the poor and the weak. Second, the evil are never finally and irredeemably condemned. Evil does lead to the anguish of fire and darkness, but God always runs out to embrace those who "come to their senses" and who turn back to God making no claim upon God's love, but asking only that relationship might be restored. They will be met with joy. And if the outwardly pious and respectable also learn the virtue of penitence, then the will and purpose of God in creation will be fully achieved, and in the kingdom of heaven there will be the fullness of joy.

Prayer
Even an unjust judge might answer the pleas of one who bothers him incessantly. Even an irritable friend may give you bread for your guests if you keep on asking. How much more will God vindicate his people who pray continually. So be

persistent in prayer. True prayer should express total reliance on God's mercy: be
like a penitent sinner, not like a self-righteous Pharisee.

Three short parables in Luke (11:5–8; 18:1–8; and 18:9–14) stress
that the right way of relating to God is by cultivating a patient,
persistent passion for justice and kindness, expressed in a life
absolutely dependent upon God, and confident that God's purposes
will ultimately be realized.

The parable of the Pharisee and the tax collector counteracts the
seeming moralism, the extreme moral rigour, of some of the parables.
It is clear that it is not conformity to the moral law which is ultimately
required of us, but an inner attitude of total dependence upon God for
whatever talents or moral strength we have. All that we have and are
belongs to God. Prayer is the surrender of what belongs to God to its
rightful owner. God's answer to such faithful and persistent prayer is
to give back into our care what we have freely offered, to be used at our
discretion to realize God's purposes.

Such prayer requires action. Speaking to God is not enough. We
must be prepared to do something to obtain justice or show compassion.
Such action carried out in conscious dependence on God *is* prayer.

The persistence of prayer is not, however, badgering God until God
does what we want. It is refusing to give in to despair, being persistent
in goodness, believing that our actions will not be in vain, and asking
for God's help in what we do, without worrying about the observable
success or failure of our actions ("Do not worry about your life",
Matthew 6:25).

Prayerful action is action without attachment to consequences. It is
action seeking to align itself to and co-operate with the will of God.
It does not aim to inform God about what God does not know. It
seeks to clarify and direct our own goals and desires, and ask for God's
help in seeing them carried out. It does not increase God's love and
compassion, but it channels it in particular ways, as a strengthening of
our love and compassion that would not have occurred without that
opening of the heart to God which invites God to act in and through
us and our thoughts and wishes.

Sometimes prayers are answered in a direct way. If prayer is opening the heart to the presence and power of God, then it enables God to act through us in new ways. We are bound together in communities, so that what we do, our moods, and our attitudes affect others. So our openness to God affects others, as our prayers for them open up new and particular forms of God's action. But not all prayers are answered as directly.

Prayers that express hatred or dislike of others, or proud, self-righteous, superior, and triumphalist attitudes with regard to others, will not be heard. Thus the prayer of the persistent widow, which is a prayer to be vindicated against her adversaries (Luke 18:3), is not the prayer of the saints of God, who pray for justice for the poor, for the triumph of goodness in the world, and for the return of all estranged creatures, including their adversaries, to God. Such prayers, which ask only for the love, reconciliation, and mercy of God, will be effective for good. When Jesus says, however, that "the Father will give you whatever you ask him in my name" (John 15:16), that is hyperbole. The requirement that we ask in the name, in the spirit of Christ who is perfect self-giving love, places limits on the sorts of prayers that will be effective, but still does not guarantee that we will receive exactly what we ask for. Jesus himself did not receive exemption from a cruel death, which he asked for in Gethsemane (Mark 14:36).

So the parables of prayer express an affirmation that we will receive the grace and power of God. Our prayer will have effect, and be used by God for good, but we cannot always tell how this will be. Yet in the world to come we will see the fruition of our prayers, and how they have been taken fully into account by God in guiding events towards the future.

In our earthly lives, through our obedience God finds new ways of acting to guide the cosmos towards its final goal. Prayer is a form of creative action and intention, but such action looks to God as its source, its sustaining strength, and its goal. It is persistent, for it should suffuse every moment of our lives. It is humble and penitent, for it seeks to make every moment consciously and wholly dependent upon God. In this sense our whole life is prayer. It is revering the majesty, beauty, and wisdom of God. It is thanking God and receiving all things at God's hands. It is placing our lives at God's disposal. And it is doing what we can to make goodness and beauty flourish in the particular circumstances that come before our attention. Prayer is communion of being with God, and it naturally seeks to include all creation in that communion. In our prayers what we should ask for, patiently and persistently, is that insofar as we can influence the course of events by thought or deed, that universal communion should be furthered. This is the prayer, the prayer of faith in the universal love of God, which God will answer without fail.

Hyperbole in the teaching of Jesus

According to Mark 11:24, Jesus said that "whatever you ask for in prayer, believe that you have received it, and it will be yours". And in Matthew 21:21, he says that "if you say to this mountain, 'be lifted up and thrown into the sea', it will be done". How can we interpret these sayings? They cannot be taken literally, or the world would be filled with permanently moving mountains, and thousands of people would be riding around in Cadillacs which they had successfully prayed for.

Perhaps it will help to remember the saying, "Faith will move mountains", which is a picturesque way of saying that things that seem impossible can become possible through faith, hope, and trusting commitment. It would be silly to take that saying literally, but it is saying something important – that you can undertake daunting tasks best by trust in the power of God.

Similarly, God will not really give us whatever we ask for. But if you ask for forgiveness, patience, the power of the Spirit, and trust wholly in God, God will support and uphold you. You have to ask for the right thing, and you may not get exactly what you ask for. But since prayer establishes communion between you and God, God will honour that communion by strengthening you in appropriate and often surprising ways.

There is an important truth here about the method Jesus uses in his teaching. He does not issue precise instructions and predictions. When he wants to commend total trust in God, he uses aphorisms that command or promise the literally impossible. Jesus puts things in a highly exaggerated way, which will have intense and memorable impact. That is hyperbole, and it is a marked feature of Jesus' teaching.

It is vitally important to keep this in mind with almost all Jesus' teachings. It would actually miss the point to take them as literal instructions or predictions. We need to seek the spiritual truth – a truth about the nature of divine–human relationship and about how humans should relate to God – underlying the difficult, even sometimes literally offensive, verbal pictures he uses.

Examples would be, "follow me, and let the dead bury their own dead" (Matthew 8:22). And, "Whoever comes to me and does not hate father and mother, wife... even life itself, cannot be my disciple" (Luke 14:26). These statements are offensive if taken literally, and would show a complete lack of sympathy for those who mourn and a contempt for family love. That is a clear indication that they should not be taken literally. Once again, you have to look for a spiritual meaning that is compatible with the loving and compassionate nature of God.

It is not too difficult to see what that meaning may be. Of course you should love your own life, for it is a gift of God. Yet you should be prepared to give it up for the sake of God and God's purpose. If there comes to be a conflict between family loyalty and God, God must prevail – but we can pray that no such conflict will arise. Just suppose that your parents wanted you to do something evil, then you should refuse. Also, you might say, to be unduly concerned about reverence for the dead instead of being concerned for bringing about good things for the future is to be trapped in desires that are not ultimately ordered to liberation and freedom from attachment. That seems to be the teaching – be free from attachments, to share in the love of God. Normally, that love will mean that you should respect the dead and love your family. But it is possible that attachment to ancestors and family might become unhealthily morbid or clinging. Thus you should seek to respect and love without clinging and morbid attachment.

Whereas the literal interpretation is offensive and incompatible with love, there is spiritual wisdom in the advice to love without attachment, and to put the pursuit of goodness before the attractions of a restricted and uncritical form of family loyalty.

An unfriendly critic could say that this sort of interpretation is an arbitrary modifying of the radical nature of Jesus' teaching. To that I would give two responses. First, a literal interpretation would be immoral, and would turn Jesus into a callous hater of families – which is unthinkable. Second, a literal interpretation would be incompatible with other central teachings – that man and wife become one flesh, for example, that you should honour your father and mother, or that you should love your neighbour as you love yourself, which means that you should not hate yourself.

I will provide just two more examples of this general, but vitally important, point about interpreting the recorded teachings of Jesus. One is the statement that "until heaven and earth pass away, not one letter, not one stroke of a letter, will pass from the law" (Matthew 5:18). Taken literally, this would endorse the most extreme form of Jewish orthodoxy, and would suggest that even the smallest regulation of the Jewish *Torah* must be obeyed "to the letter". Christians do not, however, take it in this way.

What they generally do is to take Matthew's list of laws concerning retributive justice, adultery, oath-taking, retaliation, and treatment of enemies, and concentrate attention on Jesus' interpretation of them. That interpretation gives a set of principles that cannot reasonably be taken literally. Professor Sanders suggests that in this section Jesus is saying (according to Matthew) that "the Law does not go far enough", and that Jesus "requires a stricter code of practice" from his disciples.[6] But in this case I think he underestimates the difficulty – indeed, the impossibility – of taking these "stricter rules" literally (never resisting evil, for example, or giving to anyone who asks). I suggest that Jesus is not legislating a stricter moral code, but commending a set of ideal attitudes in a hyperbolic form.

If that general principle of interpretation is established, then the "letter and stroke of a letter" statement of Matthew 5:18 must itself be interpreted by Christians as literally false for them, and as hyperbole. The meaning would then be open to a number of possible interpretations, none of which could claim to be the one true meaning of the statement. But, as I have argued, a reasonable interpretation would be that the Jewish law is and will remain forever binding on religious Jews, and it will always form an important basis for the development of a Christian morality. The law should not simply be set aside as morally irrelevant. But neither can it be retained as a set of literal instructions. For Christians, it must be transfigured by devotion to the person of Jesus and his teaching of the unlimited love of God. We must seek the underlying principles that lie behind a specific set of regulations, and ask how they can make for true human flourishing in very different cultural and historical contexts.

This brings me to the second example of hyperbole, since it is also part of the Sermon on the Mount. It is found in a slightly different form in different contexts in all Synoptic Gospels, and it is almost the only very specific-sounding moral rule that Jesus gave to his disciples. Professor Sanders cites it as "the best-attested statement of Jesus",[7] presumably because it is so shocking that nobody else would have made it up (the "principle of dissimilarity"), and it is attested in all three Synoptic Gospels (the principle of "multiple attestation"). It is Jesus' teaching on divorce and remarriage. In the Sermon, Jesus says, "Anyone who divorces his wife, except on the ground of unchastity, causes her to commit adultery; and whoever marries a divorced woman commits adultery" (Matthew 5:32).

As we would expect, this statement is literally false. A divorced woman is not an adulteress. If divorced, she is obviously no longer married, so even if she marries again she is not an adulteress. Moreover, marrying a second time is not a form of extramarital sex, and it is not destroying a functioning married relationship. So it cannot be considered to be adultery, except on the assumption that divorce is ontologically impossible; that whatever a man does, a marriage simply cannot be dissolved. This certainly conflicts with Jewish law, which allows divorce, and Jesus is supposed to be saying that every jot and tittle of the law should be observed. So there is something odd going on.

Even worse, if a woman was divorced by a man in Jewish society in Jesus' time, in order to survive she would need to get married again.

To say that it would be sinful for her to do so shows complete lack of compassion for her situation, since the divorce may not be her fault at all. Also, if anyone who marries her commits adultery, that is tantamount to saying that no man can marry a divorcee because he takes pity on her and wants to support her. That is doubly cruel. Can we really think that Jesus could have been so cruel and unthinking?

Matthew obviously does not think so, for he – alone of the Gospel editors – inserts the phrase "except on the ground of unchastity [*porneia*]". The word *porneia* means "indecency", and it reflects the Hebrew expression *ervat davar* (unclean or shameful thing) used in Deuteronomy 24:1, which gives a permissible reason for divorce in Jewish tradition (this is translated as "something objectionable" in the NRSV). Rabbinic opinion at the time of Jesus on what counted as shameful or objectionable was divided. Some rabbis (Rabbi Shammai, for example) thought that some sexual impropriety must be involved. This included adultery, but was sometimes widened to include other forms of conduct regarded as "sexually indecent". Others (such as Rabbi Hillel) were prepared to regard things that flaunted social convention as indecent, or things that could be considered offensive by the husband. There is much room for discussion about what these things might be. Hillel once proposed that burning food might count as indecent. In that context, Matthew could be opening up quite a wide field of possible exceptions to the "no divorce" rule, and allowing divorce for quite a wide variety of reasons. Could Jesus have said that, or was it just Matthew's insertion?

Professor Sanders admits that Jesus' "precise meaning is uncertain",[8] and though he seems to think that Jesus did literally prohibit divorce for his disciples, he also says that "Jesus does not say that the Mosaic regulation should be repealed", but "wishes to point his followers to a higher morality, one that corresponds to the ideal world".[9] I agree that Jesus is pointing to a higher ideal, and that he did not wish to repeal the Mosaic law. But this suggests that divorce should remain permissible, even for his disciples (since Christians are as weak or unlucky in love as Jews are!), though Jesus is saying that breaking a lifelong partnership is a failure to live out an ideal human life.

The statement about divorce has proved to be a great bone of contention for Christian churches. Not many churches have traditionally seen it as a hyperbolic statement. But the suggestion that we might do so is strengthened by the fact that it comes immediately after the recommendations that people should pull out their right eyes or cut off their right hands if they find them offensive – and hardly anyone takes these literally. Thereby it becomes part of an interpretation of the Sermon that is able to be consistent throughout, and that avoids the frequently heard charge of impossible moral perfectionism.

If it is hyperbole, then Jesus would be saying something like this: divorce is definitely wrong, and lifelong marriage should be taken very seriously. I see no reason to doubt that Jesus said this. The only question is what he meant by it. As the law says, divorce is permissible, and marriages do break down irretrievably. If and when that happens, the moral test is: "What fulfils human lives in relation to God most adequately?" not "What do these words, taken literally, command?" Beneath the hyperbolic statement is a spiritual principle, namely that partnerships founded on love are for life, and it is wrong to frustrate or destroy them. But when we fail to keep these spiritual rules, we must ask what the most humane thing to do is for all concerned.

This interpretation agrees with the way in which we interpret Jesus' other ethical statements (like "Do not resist evil", for example). It is not legalistic, but seeks the spirit of a teaching rather than a strict following of a written code – remember that such legalism is a practice which Jesus constantly criticized in the scribes and Pharisees. It avoids the charge of lack of compassion, but insists that divorce is not a trivial matter to be taken lightly, and perhaps also stresses that marriage is meant to be a deep spiritual bond between persons.

Some churches, especially the Eastern Orthodox churches, take a position not totally different from this, regarding divorce as a tragic failure to reach an ideal. But they accept that divorce is permissible for good reason, and insist that a new start, with appropriate expressions of penitence, is possible. Perhaps the most humane and compassionate course is to break the nearest thing to a literal rule that Jesus ever gave (just as we break his command not to resist evildoers) – and to do so because it expresses the compassion and humanitarian concern that Jesus showed throughout his life.

The vital principle is that we may break the literal version of moral rules given by Jesus (or by the Jewish law), precisely in order to keep the important spiritual command of loving and seeking human flourishing in relation to God, even when moral ideals have been compromised. Paying attention to this fundamental moral principle is important when considering the new moral problems that arise in our rapidly changing society. I will give just one example, which still causes deep dissent in Christian churches.

The issue of whether people of the same sex can live in lifelong loving unions and have them blessed by the church is causing much agonized discussion in Christian churches today. If we are looking to the teaching of Jesus in the New Testament, it seems fairly clear that we should support lifelong loving unions by every means at our disposal, and that the biblical prohibitions on homosexuality cannot be regarded as rules that we must follow literally. This is especially so when humanity and compassion suggest that the imposition of such rules can cause personal distress and psychological harm, and when new biological knowledge has uncovered hitherto unknown information about the biological roots of attraction and gender differences.

This does not settle the issue of whether the church can bless same-sex partnerships. Each church has the right to come to its own decisions on such matters. But I think it does establish that such blessing cannot be opposed for the simple reason that the Bible in places condemns some forms of homosexual practice. For those churches which permit divorce and remarriage in clear contradiction to a literal interpretation of almost the only new moral rule that Jesus gave, it seems inconsistent to insist on a literal interpretation of some (by no means all) Old Testament moral rules that the Gospels do not ever record Jesus as even mentioning. A consistent and compassionate interpretation of biblical moral teachings, and in particular of the recorded ethical teaching of Jesus, overrules any such biblical condemnations by asking us to seek the underlying principle of love and concern for human fulfilment in relation to God, and not to be bound by literal obedience to rules that originated in very different social conditions.

Jesus does teach ethical truths. But Jesus does not issue new moral rules. He looks to the attitudes of the heart, not to social conventions, however ancient. Attitudes of the heart are not just inner psychological states without physical expression. If they are genuine they will issue in practical action to establish justice among all peoples of the earth, and to work for a society that makes some measure of fulfilment possible for all. Nevertheless it is the attitudes of the heart of which Jesus speaks, for they are the spring from which just actions flow. Those attitudes must be attitudes of compassion, love, and concern for human flourishing. Any attitude that expresses hatred or contempt, or that is based on unreasoned though deeply rooted revulsions, must be countered by love.

My conclusion is that Jesus' moral teachings are figurative and hyperbolic forms which should not be followed in a literal way, but which express underlying spiritual teachings. These must always be compatible with unlimited divine compassion, love, and the desire that humans should find liberation from greed, pride, and hatred, and that they should flourish in conscious relationship to God.

If I have read them correctly, this group of parables outlines the ethical principles of the disciples of Jesus, the way of life of those who would be in the kingdom. The heirs to the kingdom are to be mindful, assiduous, just, humble, non-attached to wealth, compassionate, forgiving, and constant in consciousness of the presence of God. They are to be loving, joyful, peaceful, patient, kind, generous, faithful, gentle, and self-controlled. These are the qualities of mind and action that the Spirit sows and tends in the hearts of men and women that bring the kingdom near and bring life to a world estranged from the love of God.

Part 5
Theosis: The Union of Human and Divine

John's Gospel

In my account of Jesus' teachings I have concentrated on the three Synoptic Gospels. There is, of course, a fourth canonical Gospel, and it is one that cannot be ignored. A major problem is, however, that the Gospel of John is quite different in tone and style from the first three Gospels. It is a remarkable fact that in John's Gospel there are no parables, the apocalyptic teachings about the end of the age have almost disappeared, and there is no mention of Jesus' proclamation of the drawing near of the kingdom, and indeed only two mentions of the kingdom of God in the whole Gospel. The main one, at John 3:3–5, equates the kingdom with the gift of eternal life, which comes through being born of the Spirit and with believing in Jesus as Son of man. In the other (John 18:36), Jesus says to Pilate, "My kingdom is not from this world," which implies that it is not a visible, political kingdom.

It seems that talk of the kingdom of heaven is replaced, in John, with talk of eternal life. Eternal life is associated with believing in Jesus as bread of life, light of the world, the good shepherd, the resurrection, the way, the truth and the life, and the true vine. As with the Synoptic parables, these are metaphors – Jesus is not literally bread or a vine. They are, however, metaphors applied to the person of Jesus, whereas in the Synoptics most metaphors are about the nature of the kingdom.

This suggests that the kingdom is to be closely identified with the person of Jesus, and that entrance into the kingdom is by an inward spiritual union with Christ. We eat Christ's body, and we are branches of the Christ-vine. These metaphors suggest that Christ lives within us, and that we live in Christ. This is eternal life: to participate in the spiritual reality of Christ by a real communion of being. So in John the image of the disciples as members of Christ (perhaps of what Paul calls "the body of Christ" – 1 Corinthians 12:27: "you are the body of Christ and individually members of it") is central.

This teaching is never explicit in the Synoptics, and though the first three Gospels imply that the coming of the kingdom is the coming of the king, they never speak of the sort of intimate spiritual unity that resounds throughout the Gospel of John. It may be that this is the mystery at which the parables hint, but never state explicitly. So John adds another strand to the doctrine of the kingdom: the drawing near of the kingdom is the drawing near and inauguration of a new spiritual union between humans and the risen Christ; a union in which human and divine natures are united without being confused, in a new way, a way that is brought about by the gift of the Spirit, which is the gift of the ascended and glorified Christ.

The difference between the way in which Jesus speaks in the Synoptic Gospels – in parables and short cryptic aphorisms, and his telling the disciples that they should not make the truth that he is the messiah public – and the way in which Jesus speaks in the fourth Gospel – in long discourses, publicly proclaiming himself to be the Son of God – is so striking that it needs explanation.

The usual explanation, which I accept, is that the Synoptics give a more accurate picture of what Jesus is likely to have said. John, however, puts into the mouth of the earthly Jesus long theological sets of reflections on what at least one group of early churches thought the risen Jesus was. Given the testimony of the Synoptics, it is highly unlikely that Jesus ever said to the Pharisees that he was the bread of life or to the disciples that he was the true vine. Nevertheless, Mark's Gospel gives Jesus supreme authority, wisdom, and power even over nature, so such ideas may be thought to be implicit in Mark's views, though they only emerge in explicit verbal form in John.

The important point here is to see that John gives, not the actual words of Jesus, but further theological reflection on the person of Jesus from the perspective of those who knew him to have risen and to be the centre of the sacramental life of the early church. This Gospel may tell us what Jesus was and is, but it does not tell us what Jesus actually said.

Richard Bauckham has argued (in *Jesus and the Eyewitnesses*) that the Gospel of John may well be the work of an eyewitness, perhaps the work of "John the son of Zebedee", a disciple of Jesus but not one of "the Twelve". If so, this heightens the possibility that the distinctive testimony of John goes back to the earliest stratum of Christian belief, and is not some later quasi-Gnostic invention. But Professor Bauckham admits that "this testimony is idiosyncratic, and its truth is not distinguishable from its idiosyncrasy".[1] John's Gospel may not be a late invention, but it is certainly a theologically enriched account, which sees the remembered Jesus in the context of the church's experience of Jesus as risen and glorified. Perhaps John brings out what was only implicit in the Synoptic parables of Jesus. So it is possible that John expounds what was always present in Jesus' life and teaching, but whose meaning could only be seen when Jesus' ministry was completed and validated by his resurrection and ascension. As E.P. Sanders puts it, John's "work contains many teachings of the Holy Spirit, or of Jesus, who has 'come' to the author after the crucifixion and resurrection".[2]

For this reason, it is never correct to say, "Jesus, in John's Gospel, said this; so these are the actual words of Jesus." What we can say is, "John saw the person of Jesus in this way, and that has been of foundational importance for the subsequent development of views of the reality of the risen Christ."

This is not some sort of arbitrary decision about which parts of the Bible we like. It is an attempt to deal with the major discrepancy in the way Jesus speaks in the Synoptics and in John. This solution gives a deeper appreciation of the nature of all four Gospels. They do not give the exact words of Jesus. They record the way Jesus was seen by different groups of his disciples at different times. If that is so, differences of perspective are inherent in the nature of God's revelation in Jesus. Therefore such differences might be expected to persist, and indeed multiply, in contemporary churches – and they do, of course, which is partly why there are so many different churches.

Eternal life in John's Gospel

John's Gospel, like the Synoptic Gospels, contains material which can lead to an exclusive gospel of salvation for a small chosen elect group. But, like them, its leading themes proclaim the possibility of salvation for all people. This tension in John, and even more clearly in the letters of John (probably not written by the same person, but by a member of his school of thought), between exclusivism and universalism, arises from the peculiar social pressures that the Johannine community faced. As Barnabas Lindars puts it, "The Johannine church is a beleaguered sect, alienated from the local society, intensely loyal internally, but hostile to those outside. The command to love one another [John 13:34] gives a splendid example, but it does not extend to the opponents."[3]

Raymond Brown argues that John's Gospel was written in and for a rather peripheral sect that was to disappear from history as it was subsumed by the advent of the "great church".[4] It was opposed by Jews for its unequivocal assertion of the divinity of Jesus, and by other Christians for its incipiently docetic and Gnostic tendencies. That is, it could easily give rise to a denial of the full humanity of Jesus and to a doctrine of salvation by knowledge of secret teachings that were known only to a small group of initiates. In this situation, it sometimes gives the impression of being rather inward-looking and generally opposed to competing groups.

Nevertheless, Lindars goes on to say, "John was alive to this danger, and strove to prevent it. John's own understanding of the gospel message rises above sectarianism to embrace all humanity... the bounds of a nationalist faith have been broken and salvation is open to all."[5] And Raymond Brown, in his magisterial commentary on John, is at pains to point out that there are clear statements of universalism in John: Jesus takes away the sin of the world (John 1:29), not of a small group of the "elect"; Jesus draws "all men" to himself (John 12:32); and Jesus is the "saviour of the world" (John 4:42), not only of parts of the world.

John's Gospel and the letters of John do contain a definite exclusive element: those who are united in Christ have eternal life, but those who deny Christ die in their sins, and they live in a world destined for death ("You will die in your sins, unless you believe that I am he", John 8:24).

I do not think there is anything odd in saying that those who reject God's love remain in sin – in a condition of estrangement and self-destructive hatred, greed, and passion. The uncomfortable element is that the acceptance of God's love may seem to be identified exclusively with the conscious acceptance of Jesus as the messiah, and also that "dying in sin" condemns people to a changeless condemnation from which there can be no subsequent release.

The major difficulty for those who take the exclusive interpretation is that it gives a picture of God very different from that of a God who loves all creation, and who goes to the utmost lengths, even dying on the cross, to liberate humans from evil. How can such a God condemn millions of people who have never heard of Jesus, or who have never even heard that there is a God? It seems arbitrary and unfair, as well as wholly lacking in love and compassion, to condemn people for not believing something they have never heard about.

There are also a number of specific textual clues to a more positive interpretation. The quotation just given from John 8:24 is what Jesus said to the Pharisees, religious teachers who could be expected to know what the messiah was, who were confronted with the person of Jesus, who were self-righteous and self-deceiving, and who were plotting Jesus' death. That is a very specific comment to a very specific group of people, and it should not be extended to apply to people who have never even heard about Jesus.

John begins his Gospel by saying that "the Word" was with God before the universe existed, and "the Word became flesh" (John 1:14). The Word therefore cannot be confined to Jesus, even though the Word was truly embodied in the person of Jesus. It is this Word, in John's Gospel, who speaks in and through the words of Jesus, and the Word is the "I" which is referred to in the great "I am" sayings.

This interpretation is confirmed by Jesus' statement that "before Abraham was, I am" (John 8:58). The human Jesus did not exist before Abraham, and so what is being referred to is the eternal Word.

When Jesus says, "I am the true vine" (John 15:1), "abide in me as I abide in you" (15:4), he is not saying that he is a bush, or that we can somehow live inside the body of the historical Jesus. We would not want to live inside another human person, even if that made any sense. But to say that we might live in God, the spiritual being on whom the whole physical universe is founded, in conscious awareness that we are called to express the divine wisdom and compassion in our own lives, makes very good sense. To say that God might live in us is only another way of putting this desirable ideal of being interpenetrated by the divine presence and power. "Abiding in God and God abiding in us" points to an inward and intimate union of divine and human. We are no longer estranged or even apart from one another. We become particular forms in which God expresses the divine purpose, and God becomes the driving power of our lives. We are, in a sense that does not undermine our own unique individuality or the unique nature of God as creator and source of all things, one.

Thus when Jesus says he is the vine and we are the branches, he is in some sense identifying himself with God, the infinite and eternal being who underlies and is present to the whole universe. The human Jesus speaks, but in and through him speaks the eternal Word of God, and it is that infinite and unbounded Word of which he speaks. It would be virtually blasphemy to identify this Word, existent before all worlds, completely and without qualification with the human Jesus. We must live in the eternal Word, which is truly expressed in Jesus but not confined to that one human mind and body. When we see this clearly, we will no longer be tempted to think that God limits salvation to those who knew the historical Jesus, or who have met his disciples. God offers salvation to all through the eternal Word, and that Word is present at every time and place, in forms we may not recognize. But the Christian claim is that if we would know what that Word really is, we can find it humanly expressed in Jesus.

That is why it is wrong to identify the Word by which all beings are united to God simply and without qualification to the human Jesus. In a similar way, it is unnecessary to think that people must decide their eternal relationship to God before they die, and that after death it is too late to repent. The Word is "the true light which enlightens everyone" (John 1:8), and thus may be known in some manner to all people. It is by that encounter, hidden in the depths of each human heart, that all will be judged. The true nature of that encounter, and the fuller revelation of the truth that it is indeed the Word of God that was truly expressed in Jesus that was encountered, may come after death. Learning and deciding may come after death.

John 5:25 says, "The hour is coming, and is now here, when the dead will hear the voice of the Son of God." Those who have died will hear Christ, even if they did not do so during their earthly lives. People do not have to hear of Christ before they die; the important meeting with Christ may be after death.

John's Gospel continues: "all who are in their graves will hear his voice and will come out – those who have done good, to the resurrection of life, and those who have done evil, to the resurrection of condemnation" (John 5:28–29). The dead are not judged according to their faith in Jesus, but according to whether they have done good or evil. A similar idea is found at Acts 10:35: "in every nation anyone who fears him [God] and does what is right is acceptable to him". There is no explicit mention of Christ here, and acceptability to God apparently depends almost entirely on being just, not in specific faith in Jesus.

These passages may trouble some Christians, who (rightly) think that people can be saved only by faith and not by works. But of course there is a twist to these narratives. In fact there is a double twist. First, is anyone truly good? Second, are people not in fact saved by faith in Christ? – "by this Jesus everyone who believes is set free from all those sins from which you could not be freed by the law of Moses" (Acts 13:39).

This tension of salvation by works or by faith has been a perennial theme of Christian debate throughout the centuries. I do not expect to be able to end that debate in a sentence or two. But one resolution of the tension is to say that people are acceptable to God if they do what is just. But only God can "save" them, bring them into intimate loving union with God. God does this by bringing them to personal encounter with Jesus Christ. The decisive point is that Jesus does not save only the just. Jesus offers eternal life to all who, upon meeting him, repent and believe in him, whether they have been truly just or not.

If this is so, then when the dead hear the voice of Christ, when they truly meet him for the first time, they hear the voice of one who condemns their injustice. But they also hear one who offers forgiveness and eternal life. The "resurrection of condemnation" is not to a state beyond the possibility of release. For the voice that condemns is also, and decisively, a voice that offers life and an opportunity, perhaps for the first time for them, to follow the Christ they never properly knew until that encounter.

John's Gospel, then, may be taken to suggest that all people will truly encounter Christ beyond death. And all will then make a decisive choice to accept or reject the divine love as it exists in him. But that is not a reason to defer any such decision until after death. In fact if anyone consciously does that, they are in effect rejecting Christ by refusing the transformation of life that God now offers. Even that will not inevitably condemn anyone forever. But it will harden the heart against God's love, and it will increase the torments of self-hatred and anguish that have been symbolized by traditional images of hell. Hell may not be endless; but whether endless or not, it is a state to be feared. More importantly, it is a state which prevents any sharing in the joyful feast of the kingdom and any vision of the beauty and majesty of God.

John's Gospel is a Gospel of sharply drawn contrasts. It contrasts death and life, the world and the spirit, darkness and light. Eternal life is life in companionship with the eternal, and it brings light and joy. Eternal death is life estranged from the eternal, and it is lived in darkness and misery. There is, I think, an important asymmetry between eternal life and eternal death, an asymmetry which follows from the unchanging nature of God as redemptive love. Eternal life, once gained, cannot be lost, for it is unthinkable that anyone who has found the treasure of life with God would turn away. But eternal death, being a state of misery, is something most of us would turn away from if we could. There is in fact something odd in speaking of "eternal destruction", since once something is destroyed, it ceases to be. This implies that, while eternal life is unending joy, eternal death is simply non-existence.

These passages suggest that there is a possibility of "eternal death", complete non-existence, ceasing to be. But there is also a possibility of "eternal life", life fulfilled in the invincible love of God. There is little talk in John's Gospel of suffering in hell. There is just the stark contrast of life or death, and a stress that Christ comes to give life and to save from death, not to judge or condemn. John does contrast very sharply "the world", which is ruled by the devil, which hates the disciples and is doomed to destruction, from the "light", which is true life in the Spirit. But John also stresses that the Christ comes to save, to redeem, the world. This implies that salvation is not limited to those who explicitly confess Jesus as Lord, and to those who do so before they die. Christ is the way, the truth, and the life, by whom all must finally come to God. But intelligent souls may encounter Christ in many hidden ways, and many will not encounter Christ as he truly is until after their earthly life is over. Being open to truth, goodness, and beauty is, from the Christian point of view, being open to the "light that lightens every one", which is revealed in its fullness in Jesus.

That is perhaps why John's Gospel no longer speaks of an imminent return of Christ in glory. It is not so much that, as Rudolf Bultmann suggested in his *The Gospel of John*, the few passages which speak of future judgment are later additions to John's original Gospel. It may rather be that the kingdom – the entrance into eternal life – will not fully come until all have had the opportunity to encounter the glorified Christ, and for many millions of souls that will not happen until after death. The change of perspective from a hope for the restoration of a national monarchy for Israel to a hope for the uniting of the whole cosmos to God was critical for the development of the Christian faith into a truly universal religion. In John's Gospel the move is made from thinking of the kingdom of God as an earthly monarchical rule in Jerusalem to the idea of eternal life as the spiritual destiny of the whole world.

In my view, John emphasizes an important element in the teaching
of Jesus, partly concealed in the metaphors of the Davidic kingdom,
and partly misunderstood by some of his disciples in a literalist way
as an observable ending of history in the near future. John understood
Jesus more adequately as a teacher of universal significance for the
spiritual renewal of the earth. Even John perhaps did not always see
clearly the truly universal implications of his Gospel and sometimes
held a more introverted and exclusive view that confined the love of
God to one small "elect" community. While both the universal and
the exclusive views may be present in John's Gospel, the magnificent
"Prologue" (chapter 1) unequivocally gives the universal view – that
Jesus' life expresses the universal and unlimited love of God for all
creation – priority.

The threefold God of John's Gospel

As John presents the teaching of Jesus, God is not pictured as an
eternal and unchanging Other who is unaffected by all the things
that happen in the universe. This is "the God of the philosophers",
described by Aristotle, and inscribed in the philosophical works
of Thomas Aquinas. Nor is God pictured as an all-determining
sovereign who treats humans as subjects who simply have to be
obedient to divine authority and power. This is the God of
monarchical theism, who is wholly other than the created world
and determines it to be what it is by eternal and changeless decree.
Rather, God is pictured as a supreme spiritual reality with whom
creatures are, or are to become, one. Jesus prays to the Father "that
they may be one, as we are one, I in them and you in me, that they
may become completely one" (John 17:20–21). The Father is in
Christ, and Christ is in the believers. Moreover, "I am in my Father,
and you in me, and I in you" (John 14:20). Believers are in Christ,
and Christ is in the Father. Furthermore, "the Spirit… abides with
you, and he will be in you" (John 14:17). The Spirit too, "sent" by
Christ, dwells in believers.

These passages may be mysterious, and they are certainly
metaphorical. Yet they seem to deny that the Father, the Son, the

Spirit, and believers, are all separate entities. There is a mutual indwelling of Father, Son, Spirit, and the redeemed. The redeemed live in God, and God, as Father, Son, and Spirit, lives in the redeemed. The teaching is not that God is separate from human souls, but that God and souls live "in" each other. We live in God, and God lives within us. Individual selves do not, however, disappear into some sort of divine undifferentiated unity. They find their true fulfilment when they are so united in God that they have access to the infinite experience, wisdom, and power of God, and when God feels and acts in and through them in unique ways.

These images suggest that the created world is not something fully external to God that leaves God quite unchanged. The incarnation of the Word in Jesus, and the abiding of Christ and the Spirit in the lives of men and women, involves God in the created world in a dynamic and intimate way. We might even think of creation as an expression of the infinite reality of God, which enables God to realize the divine nature in and through the lives of finite creatures. In the history of Christian thought, that idea was perhaps not fully formulated until the genesis of the sort of philosophical idealism that is found in Hegel. Yet it seems an intelligible development of the Johannine writings to think of the goal of creation as the actualization of Spirit expressed in a communion of love.

The modern Greek Orthodox theologian John Zizioulas speaks of the being of God as "being as communion", and suggests, in line with much modern thought, that persons are fulfilled in relationship. Only as persons stand in relationships of love to one another can they express a truly personal form of being. Zizioulas argues that the internal relations of the persons within the Trinity enable being as communion to exist. Yet the persons of the Trinity, in most Orthodox theologies, are inseparable and indefectible – they cannot be alienated from one another, and cannot take independent courses of action. Thus God's creation of truly autonomous and independent persons, with real moral and creative freedom, would enable another form of personal relationship to exist. In that form, there would be the risk of falling away and of a breaking of relationship, but also the possibility of reconciliation and the restoration of a deeper union of love.

We may thus picture a world of autonomous persons who turn from God, of a God who renounces changeless bliss to enter into that world and reconcile it to the divine love, and of a transfiguration of the world in which finite creatures are taken beyond the transience of time, so that all their temporal experiences, their struggles, defeats, and victories, are inscribed forever in a form transfigured by the glorious infinity of the divine being. That picture seems to me to be an authentic development – even, I would say, a strong implication – of John's affirmation that Father, Son, Spirit, and the redeemed, are "in" each other, or are "one" in a sense undefined by John. That unity will fulfil, not negate, personal selfhood, but it will affirm that such fulfilment is only attained within a wider communion of personal being. In such communion, each personal being is changed in mutual responsiveness and creative action.

It is perhaps odd, in the face of this teaching, how nervous Christians have often been when they hear the word "pantheism". Of course, if that word means that God is nothing more than the material universe, then it is grossly inadequate. But if it means that God and the world are intimately bound together, as one reality, that seems to be what John's Jesus is saying. We rightly emphasize that God is infinitely more than the material world, and that the world is not at all omniscient and omnipotent and perfect in being. In modern theology, the word "panentheism", coined by Karl Krause in nineteenth-century Germany, is sometimes used to make this emphasis apparent. We and our world will always be infinitely less than God, but there will be a real and deep communion of being between God and the redeemed cosmos. The infinite and the finite, the eternal and the temporal, will be united. And this unity is anticipated and foreshadowed in the person of Jesus, in whom Christian doctrine sees divine and human natures as indissolubly united.

Yet at the same time John's Gospel makes a very clear distinction between "the world" and "eternal life". That is one reason why Christians faithful to biblical tradition have been wary of the word "pantheism". They are well aware that the world is a realm of darkness, into which Christ breaks as light which brings liberation, and it is a realm of death, into which Christ breaks as a bringer of life. So the full unity of divine and human for which Jesus prays, and which his life anticipates, is a future reality rather than a present one. It is partly found in the lives of those who now live in Christ, but they (even when you include those touched by Christ without consciously recognizing it) are perhaps a small minority in the world as a whole. There may be a future unity, but the present is a duality of good and evil in which Christ comes in self-sacrificial love to reconcile and make one what is torn apart by greed, hatred, and violence.

Jesus says, "The bread that I will give is my flesh, which I will give for the life of the world" (John 6:51). God enters into time in a kenotic, self-sacrificial way in order to reconcile the estranged world to the divine being. Jesus is not someone who gives commands that have to be obeyed on pain of death. Jesus eats and drinks with outcasts, forgives and reconciles, and offers eternal life to those who are lost in the darkness of the world. If they turn away, they remain in darkness, and that is the judgment. Yet Jesus is "the Lamb", whose life is sacrificed, not for a select few, but for "the sin of the world" (John 1:29). The world may be estranged from God, but God acts in Christ – and that universal action is definitively expressed in Jesus – to reconcile it to its true ground in God.

John's Gospel does not explicitly address the question of how the world came to be in darkness. But there is no question that John accepts the basic prophetic doctrine of the creation of the world by God for the sake of goodness: "The world came into being through him [the Word], yet the world did not know him" (John 1:10). I think the best clue to John's view is found in the first letter of John, widely thought to be by the editor of the Gospel or at least by a member of the Johannine community: "God is love" (1 John 4:9). God's love is a sacrificial love that seeks to give life to others. God's love is even "perfected in us" (1 John 4:12). The word translated as "perfected" is *teteleiomene*, and it has the sense of something being fulfilled, or accomplishing its goal.

That suggests that the purpose of God in creation is that the divine nature as self-giving love should be perfected by its coinherence in creatures, by a communion of being between infinite and created life. The divine nature itself is perfected by creation. Arguably, this means that the creation of creatures capable of being filled with the divine love is in a sense part of the completion of the divine nature. It is not that God is compelled by some external necessity to create. God's own nature necessarily issues in creation, since God's nature is self-giving love, which therefore by nature wills to create others who can receive and share that love.

If, however, God creates that which is truly other – personal beings who have their own autonomous choices – then it is understandable that they may choose self-centred and egoistic lives rather than lives that acknowledge their total dependence upon God, and their need to live in co-operation with others. The relation of God to such a cosmos is creative, relational, and dynamic. God creates and leaves free. God works within creation without determining what happens in it, but in a way which seeks to guide and inspire, to reconcile persons to the divine. And God fulfils creation, and even, the word *teteleiomene* breathtakingly suggests, fulfils the divine nature itself, by taking creation into the divine and eternal life, where the history of the cosmos will find its apotheosis.

There is a distinctive picture of God in John's Gospel, and it is very different from pictures of God as a remote and unchanging First Cause, or as an all-determining monarch. It is no accident that the metaphor of Jesus as king does not play a major part in the Gospel. It is replaced by the metaphors of Jesus as bread and wine, the true vine, and the way to life. The picture is of a God whose being is authentically expressed in a cosmic narrative of creation, relation, self-giving, reconciliation, and fulfilment. The history of the cosmos is part of the history of God, who is essentially creative, relational, and unitive. That is the God of Israel, who, according to the prophet Hosea, said to Israel, "You will call me 'my husband'… and I will take you for my wife for ever" (Hosea 2:16, 19). John's Gospel deepens that ancient prophetic image of a marriage in which two people become "one flesh" (Genesis 2:24), and depicts God and the redeemed as mutually indwelling, as "one" in an even more interior way. It is quite difficult to read this and not to think that the history of God and the cosmos are bound together in an intimate and quasi-personal way.

God as primordial, expressive, and unitive being

The Anglican theologian John Macquarrie proposed a set of concepts which seems to me to express this picture very helpfully. The being of God is threefold. It has three modes of being, which are not reducible to one another, and all of which are essential to the divine nature. These modes Macquarrie called the primordial, the expressive, and the unitive modes of the divine being.

In twentieth-century theology, Jürgen Moltmann and Wolfhart Pannenberg developed somewhat similar threefold analyses of the idea of God. All these analyses have their philosophical source in the work of Hegel, who spoke of the three modes of *Geist*, or "Absolute Spirit", as "being-in-itself" (the primordial), "being-for-itself" (the expressive), and "being-in-and-for itself" (the unitive). It should not be thought, however, that theologians are just using a wholly independent philosophical vocabulary. For Hegel, himself a Lutheran Christian, thought he was developing a truly Christian philosophy. Whether or not that was the case, his work has been immensely important for subsequent theology, especially, though not only, for Protestant theology.

Each theologian develops the analysis in a rather different way, but Macquarrie's work is especially helpful for those, like Karl Barth and Karl Rahner, who stress the unity of one consciousness and will in God, and speak of the Trinity as something like "three ways of being as God", or three modalities of the divine being, rather than as a union of three different personal agencies. Jesus (according to Mark) said, repeating Deuteronomy 6:4: "The Lord our God, the Lord is one" (Mark 12:29). In accordance with this statement, Macquarrie stresses the unity of the being of God more strongly than either Pannenberg or Moltmann, though without denying an essential threefoldness in the divine being.

For John Macquarrie, the primordial mode of being is that which is the ultimate source of all creation, and which is necessarily and eternally existent. It cannot fail to exist and its general nature cannot be other than it is. It exists beyond time and space, so it cannot logically be brought into being, changed, impaired, or destroyed. It is this aspect of the divine being that Aquinas's definitions of God in the *Summa Theologiae* describe. But this mode of being does not give a complete description of God, and it is in itself incomplete. For God is also essentially expressive or creative, and the primordial nature of God needs to be expressed so that the love of God (which is God's primordial nature) can be "perfected", as John's first letter puts it.

God is necessarily and changelessly "love". It is the divine essence to be related in love to others, and, since it is the one and only source of all being, to create others. Freedom is essential to love, since love cannot be compelled or determined by another. Therefore the creation of others entails the possibility of estrangement, of their seeking self-determination in freedom, a self-determination which can even cast aside the love which is the true source of their existence. A created cosmos is contingent. It is not necessarily what it is, for in it beings can choose to live well or badly, and whichever they choose, they could do otherwise. What they do, they do not do by necessity.

Now, however, there is a puzzle. How can a God who is necessary bring into being a cosmos that is contingent, since whatever a necessary being brings about must itself be necessary (there can be no alternative to what such a being does)? The resolution of the puzzle is simple but profound. God is necessary in some but not in all respects.

God is necessary in respect of the divine existence, as the source of all being. God is necessary in being the source of all power and in possessing the greatest degree of power that any being could possibly possess (that is, I think, an adequate definition of omnipotence, though it does not entail that God could do anything we can consistently describe). God is necessary in possessing the greatest degree of knowledge any being could possibly possess (that is omniscience, knowing everything that is possible and everything that is actual). God is necessary in possessing the greatest degree of goodness or value that any being could possibly possess, and, if contingent beings are created, in creating them for the sake of the unique forms of goodness they may generate (the divine being is perfect, and creates for the sake of good). This is because an omniscient and omnipotent mind will know what is truly good, and will choose to actualize possible states for the sake of their goodness.

God is an eternal and necessary mind (since only minds know and have purposes) that is omnipotent, omniscient, and of supreme value. But (and this is what even Aquinas did not fully or explicitly recognize) precisely because God is omnipotent (has the potential to do many things) and of supreme value (which is love), God is also necessarily creative, relational, and loving. For, as the revelation of God in Christ shows us, the supreme perfection is love, and love requires the creation of otherness, of contingency, of the possibility of estrangement, and it motivates self-sacrificial action to reconcile and fulfil the possibilities of a communion of persons in God.

Thus the primordial being of God necessarily moves out of itself in order fully to express its nature. The expressive mode of divine being is the contingent creative mode of action of an eternal and necessary mind. If God is truly to be named "Father", and if that is part of the divine nature, then God necessarily has "children", persons with their own autonomy. It may be a contingent matter which free creatures God creates, how they act specifically, and how God responds to those actions. But it seems that some such creation is part of the divine nature as love. And some values are such that they cannot exist without the existence of some suffering and frustration, and without the possibility of much more, if freedom is misused.

When, as in our world, it has been misused, that world enters into a darkness and self-destructiveness from which there is no escape without divine help. "The world" will seem to be in opposition to the eternal life of God, and a return to God will only be possible if God actively enters into the world to redeem it. So the world is or is meant to be the expression of the divine nature. But in its otherness and plurality it has fallen away from its divine origin, and the images of God in the world, in its beauty and intelligibility, its possibilities for individual creativity and social relationships, have become blurred and ambiguous. In such a "fallen" world God may create a more perfect image of the divine being. Christians believe that in the person of Jesus there is the true "image of the invisible God" (Colossians 1:15), and by that image the world may be restored to its true function of being a moving image and sacrament of eternity.

Life in "the world" is life directed by self-centred desires, by ambition, the lust for power, and competition with others. Life "in Christ" is life directed by self-giving love, by concern with the flourishing of all creatures, as far as it is possible, and by love of the good-and-beautiful, wherever it is found, and supremely in God, the ultimate origin and goal of all beings.

The unitive mode of the divine being is that by which all things are reconciled in God, and come to be "participants in the divine nature" (2 Peter 1:4). Here all evil and suffering are either eliminated or transformed into a fully realized form of goodness that could not otherwise have existed. That is the perfecting of divine love, and the consummation of creation.

There is a more than accidental correspondence between the Christian doctrine of God as Father, Son, and Spirit, and this analysis of the divine being as primordial, expressive, and unitive. For Christian faith, God the Father is the ultimate source of all created being. God the Son is how the divine nature is expressed in the creation of a community of personal beings, and Jesus is the authentic image in human form of the objective expression of the divine nature. God the Spirit is the reconciling and unitive action of God throughout creation, patterned on the life of Jesus, which transfigures finite lives so that they become one with the divine.

The astonishing picture that John's Gospel provides is that this threefold being of God is worked out in the history of creation. It is not something that belongs to the hidden and timeless nature of God, whether or not there is a universe (the so-called "immanent Trinity").

Of such a thing I do not think we can dare to speak, nor have we any licence to do so. Some theologians have suggested that unless we know that God's *ousia*, God's innermost being, is Trinitarian in form, then our knowledge that God's being is Trinitarian in relation to us (the *economia* of God) must be incomplete, inadequate, or even false. This is not so. It may be that God's being-in-itself is unknown to human minds, yet God's being is truly expressed in relation to us. The appearance is not false, for God is truly expressed as fully as is possible for finite human minds. Appearance is not illusion. Thus it is perfectly coherent to say that God's being-in-itself is largely unknown and unknowable, but it is such that it is truly expressed in Trinitarian form in relation to us.

What is sometimes called "Rahner's Rule", that the immanent Trinity is identical to the economic Trinity,[6] is not compelling if it means that God's being-in-itself must be exactly the same as God's being-as-it-relates-to-us. I think it would be very odd if this were so, for it would commit us to a form of naive realism about human knowledge that would not be generally accepted in the realm of scientific and commonsense knowledge. When, for example, we see the world as an array of three-dimensional solid coloured objects, we do not see falsely. We see truly what the material universe of possibly ten-dimensional wave particles is in relation to our forms of perception. But the reality, when it is unperceived, is something very different. How much more might we expect this to be true of God, whose essential being is beyond any adequate human understanding.

What we can say, perhaps, is that God's being-in-itself is truly expressed in the only way we can understand, and as fully and adequately as we can understand it, in Trinitarian form. And that understanding requires us to think of God as truly – not in an ephemeral or illusory way – expressed in the history of the cosmos. God truly has a history, and though God's being transcends history, that is something of which we cannot speak.

What the Gospel of John suggests to me is that God perfects the divine love in the narrative of cosmic history, so that the Trinity becomes a dynamic process involving both God and the cosmos –

and that process is our clue to what God essentially is: the necessary source of all, who enters into creation to enable it to find fulfilment by participation in the divine nature. The pattern of the divine life is a threefold pattern of *kenosis*, *henosis*, and *theosis*: self-sacrificial love, the unity of finite and infinite being (on this planet, the unity of divinity and humanity in Christ), and the raising of the finite to participate in the divine. That pattern is worked out in the history of the cosmos when the cosmos is seen in all its spiritual depth.

Am I seriously suggesting that Jesus taught this complex and profound interpretation of cosmic history? No, Jesus was not taking a philosophy class, and it is significant that he did not write a philosophy book. But I am arguing that John's Gospel does suggest such a philosophical scheme, at least in embryonic form. It sees Jesus as the cosmic Word by whom the cosmos was created, from whom the cosmos turned away, who entered into the cosmos to reunite it to God, and in whom the whole of creation is to be reconciled and united. Perhaps the clearest expression of such a view, and one that may well pre-date John's Gospel, is found in the letter to the Colossians: "In him all things in heaven and on earth were created... and in him all things hold together... and through him God was pleased to reconcile to himself all things, whether on earth or in heaven" (Colossians 1:15–20). Such thoughts are not confined to John, but form the background to some New Testament letters, and therefore were current in the early church.

Spiritual metaphor in the teachings of Jesus

I have attempted to understand the nature of Jesus' teaching by an internal study of the New Testament parables and other sayings of Jesus. They must strike any attentive student as exceedingly dramatic, highly metaphorical, often hugely paradoxical and sometimes shatteringly blunt, judgmental, and impossibly demanding. Yet they are uttered by a person who "has not come to destroy the lives of human beings but to save them" (Luke 9:56, only in some ancient manuscripts), and who came "to serve, and to give his life a ransom for many" (Mark 10:45).

I have claimed that we should not take Jesus' teachings literally as describing physical events, sometimes events which will happen on or near our earth and in the near future. It may be helpful to review a few examples to amplify this claim a little further. According to Mark's Gospel, Jesus at his trial before the high priest said, "You will see the Son of man seated at the right hand of the Power, and coming with the clouds of heaven" (Mark 14:62). God has no physical body and therefore no right-hand side. Jesus is not sitting down by his side. And Jesus is not going to come in a sort of divine helicopter, piloted presumably by God, descending through the clouds. He is certainly not going to be physically observed to do so – he was never literally observed in that way by the high priest to whom he made this statement.

We could not even plausibly say that Jesus meant his statement literally, but just turned out to be mistaken (since the high priest never saw him in the clouds), for Jesus, as a Jew, knew very well that God had no physical body (though God had appeared in visions in human form). But there is no reason to insist on a literal and physical interpretation. We are perfectly familiar with the expression that a person may sit at your right hand metaphorically – meaning that he is your "right-hand man", the one who might be relied on to carry out your desires efficiently or who can act with your authority.

So for Jesus to sit at God's right hand, or to sit on a glorious throne, is really to say that he will be seen to possess divine authority and will be fully vindicated as king of Israel by God. When Jesus ascends to heaven, he does not physically rise through the clouds to find God high in the sky. The ascension is the assumption of divine authority in the glory of the Father. The physical image is a symbol for Jesus' vindication by God, and the beginning of his everlasting kingship in glory.

It is consonant with such a symbolic interpretation to see the cloud of God's presence, the *Shekinah*, as the "cloud of unknowing" that surrounds and symbolizes the divine being-present, the *parousia*. "Coming with the clouds" would then not be a physical description of a future event in Jerusalem. It could symbolize the presence of Christ in glory in the community of the new covenant, in which Christ is enthroned as king (in which he rules, spiritually). It may seem unlikely that the Synoptic writers had this interpretation in mind, though it is hard to know how metaphorically they were using the language they had. I think however that, even if they had some literal description in mind, the important teaching would be about the status of the glorified Christ in relation to God. And that teaching remains, even when the literal description has been lost.

In that case, Jesus would not be saying to the high priest that he would soon observe some paranormal celestial phenomenon. Jesus would be saying that the priest, who is now colluding in Jesus' passion and death, will in fact still be living when that same Jesus ascends to the glory of the Father and is enthroned as Lord of the church.

Jesus' assertion is framed in physical, material, literal terms. It is what I have called a spiritual metaphor, for while it is false if taken in a physical sense, it conveys a truth about heavenly things in earthly images. Heavenly things are facts both about the present and about the future, not mere pieces of poetry without any claim to objective truth, or merely statements about some purely subjective states. But these facts are not physical facts. They are spiritual facts, about Jesus' relation to God and to God's purpose in the redemption of the world, and about our relation to the risen Lord.

Spiritual facts are about human states of consciousness, but about such states insofar as they relate to the objective realities of other persons and to God. In this world, such states are often hidden, but in the world to come, they will be openly expressed in some form: "Whatever you have said in the dark will be heard in the light" (Luke 12:3). We may not be able to imagine what that form is, and we can only speak of it in the physical terms we know. So Jesus really exists after death, but we do not know where or in what form of body. He really is enthroned as king, but we cannot imagine what the public expression of that kingship will be like (see 1 John 3:2: "What we will be has not yet been revealed. What we do know is this: when he is revealed, we will be like him, for we will see him as he is"). That is because spiritual truths are about human lives in God, and though we may think there must be some shared, public expression of that form of existence, we have no idea what it will be (see also 1 Corinthians 15:35–38: "someone will ask... 'With what kind of body do they [the resurrected dead] come?' Fool!... God gives it a body as he has chosen").

There are many examples of such spiritual metaphors in the Gospels. Matthew applies a quotation from Isaiah 53:4 to Jesus: "He took our infirmities and bore our diseases" (Matthew 8:17). It is false that Jesus literally had the diseases that he cured in others, and Matthew means only that Jesus cured those who were sick. Yet there is a deeper spiritual meaning. The cures were real, but what they show is that God enters into the human and God-estranged world in order to reunite it to God. The literally false image that Jesus had our diseases expresses the spiritual truth that, by his self-sacrificial love and union with us, he heals the infirmity of egoism and unites us to God. That spiritual meaning remains true even for those whom Jesus does not physically heal. The physical healings were extraordinary expressions of Jesus' unique relation to God and his unique role in religious history. Spiritual healing, liberation from hatred and greed by the touch of the Spirit, is what the Gospels are mainly concerned with.

Again, in Matthew 11:14, Jesus says that "he [John the Baptist] is Elijah who is to come". Few theologians, if any, believe that Jesus meant this literally, as though Elijah had reincarnated in the Baptist. The reference is to Malachi 4:5: "I will send you the prophet Elijah before the great and terrible day of the Lord comes." Luke gets it right when he says that the Baptist will come with "the spirit and power of Elijah" (Luke 1:17). Saying that the Baptist is Elijah is a spiritual metaphor which makes the point that the Baptist prepares the way for the advent of the Son of man, who brings the kingdom of God near.

A final example is Jesus' reported saying, "I watched Satan fall from heaven like a flash of lightning. See, I have given you authority to tread on snakes and scorpions" (Luke 10:18–19). A literal reading would be that Jesus physically saw a demonic being tumbling from the sky, and that the disciples could tread on snakes without being harmed. It would be both misleading and dangerous to accept such a literal reading and go about treading on snakes just to demonstrate its truth.

In fact these are images taken from Old Testament passages, and we must begin by going back to those sources. Isaiah 14:12 reads: "How you are fallen from heaven, O Day Star, son of Dawn!" This is indeed a reference to Satan, but Isaiah is using it to refer to the downfall of the king of Babylon. The fall of the Day Star – Satan, the heavenly power – is equated with the fall of the military power that had taken Israel into exile. Presumably Satan did not fall from heaven twice, so it seems clear that Jesus is using the imagery of Satan in a similar way, to speak of the downfall of oppressive spiritual powers that have led humanity into exile and captivity – exile from God and captivity to egoistic desire. There was not a demon tumbling through the air. There was the overthrow of powers that separate humanity from God, powers of hatred, greed, and pride. That is what Jesus saw as the seventy disciples reported the success of their mission.

As for treading on snakes and scorpions, Psalm 91:13 reads: "You will tread on the lion and the adder, the young lion and the serpent you will trample under foot." The details of this psalm are literally false – those "who live in the shelter of God" will not be preserved from all harm – Jesus himself suffered a cruel death. The psalm is a poetic hymn of hope in the ultimate spiritual protection of God. It states in poetic hyperbole that God will deliver us out of all our troubles. That is ultimately and spiritually true. Just as Jesus was resurrected, and so triumphed over death, so may we do so if we trust in God. But this does not literally mean that we shall never suffer any troubles, or even disasters.

This is a case, then, where a literal interpretation is actually rather naive. What is put in metaphorical and hyperbolic terms is that evil will be defeated and we will live with God, and that this defeat and protection begin now as we encounter and begin to be transformed by the Spirit of Jesus. The disciples would have known and understood these Old Testament references to the overcoming of egoism and the liberating power of God. But to understand them truly we have to see that they are not literal descriptions, but profound spiritual metaphors.

These are only a few examples which lead me to say that many of Jesus' teachings are spiritual metaphors or symbols framed in terms of physical – observable and public – things and events, but meant to refer to spiritual states and possibilities – states presently unobservable and inner, but destined to be openly known when, after death, we share fully in the life of God.

If that is true in some cases, it is important to know whether it is true of most or all cases, or only of some. The New Testament text does not carry little messages saying, "The next bit is metaphorical." So the Bible does not answer that question. My view is that almost all the central teachings of Jesus are framed in metaphorical terms, but each reader has to judge that for themselves.

What are the central teachings of Jesus? I think they come down to four. First, there is judgment, especially of hypocrites, the proud, and the greedy. Second, there is forgiveness, especially of the just and merciful, of repentant sinners, and of those who receive Jesus with joy. Third, there is a new community of the Spirit of God, a new age of religious life, when the disciples of Jesus are called to act as his body on earth. Fourth, there is the final consummation of all things when everything in heaven and earth will be united in Christ, and share fully in the divine nature. Jesus, as Son of man – a human life perfectly fulfilled in God – rules in this community, both in earth and in heaven, as one who serves, and in it the union of humanity and divinity is now being progressively and often hesitantly, but inevitably, forged.

The Gospels of John and Thomas on the teaching of Jesus

Since I believe that Jesus rose from death and ascended to the presence of God, and that his presence is still known in the church through the Spirit, I will with good reason give a high degree of authority to the recorded teachings of Jesus that have been accepted as authoritative by the church. I will be disposed to think that the central themes of his teaching are correct, and originate in a deeper and wider understanding of God's nature and purposes than I have, or anyone else has. I will think that the Christian churches have not fallen into fundamental error about Jesus' person and teachings.

This does not mean, however, that I will accept every recorded teaching of Jesus in the Gospels as verbally accurate, just as it stands. Indeed, I cannot do so, since I am aware of differing accounts of Jesus' sayings in differing Gospels. There are also "gospels" like the Gospel of Thomas, which were not accepted as authoritative by the church, but which were sometimes referred to by early Christian writers and given some authority by them.

The Gospel of Thomas is the most interesting of the non-canonical gospels, and should be considered in any attempt to examine Jesus' teaching. I am, however, glad that this Gospel, discovered in the Nag Hammadi caves in 1945, did not become part of the canon of Scripture. It ends with the statement, "Every woman who makes herself male will enter the kingdom of Heaven" (logion 114), a sentiment with which I heartily disagree. But Thomas, self-described as a set of "secret" teachings of Jesus, contains many sayings that are found in the canonical Gospels, in an interestingly different form. It contains some sayings about the kingdom of heaven which are rather different in tone from those in the Synoptic Gospels. In a variant of a saying found in Luke, it says, "The kingdom is within you and it is without you" (logion 3). More cryptic is the saying, "Blessed are the solitary and elect, for you shall find the kingdom because you came from it, and you shall go there again" (logion 50). This seems to express a Gnostic or Neoplatonic thought that human souls descend into the world from a heavenly realm, and by secret knowledge and solitary contemplation they may ascend to the heavenly realm again.

A similar thought that the kingdom is not in an earthly future, but in a spiritual present, seems to be expressed in some sayings: "When will the new world come? He said to them: what you expect has come, but you know it not" (logion 51). And "The kingdom of the Father is spread upon the earth and men do not see it" (logion 113).

What I think this shows is that there was in existence from quite early times a Platonic interpretation of Jesus' teachings. The general picture of human life is very like the one described by Plato in his parable of the cave.

Humans are bound in a deep cavern, facing the rear wall. On that wall they see shadows of puppets placed behind them, shadows cast by the light of a fire placed between them and the cave entrance. The prisoners take these shadows to be real things, but in fact they are at two removes from reality. They are shadows, and they are cast by puppets, not by real persons. If a prisoner escapes from the cave, he will see the sun and real figures moving around in a world of light and freedom. But if he returns to the cave and reports what he has seen, this will seem so strange to those bound in the cave that he will not be believed.[7]

For Plato, the way to escape from the cave is by training in mathematics and dialectical philosophy, which culminates in an intellectual vision of the intelligible world, at the apex of which is the idea of the Good. In the Christian story, this intellectual training is replaced by training in practical love. The wisdom of God is the wisdom of love, not of theoretical understanding. This wisdom, the Logos, enters the darkness of our world, where people's desires are centred on things which are unreal, insecure, and transient, and where we see only facades of the self that people present to others, and not the innermost centres of their personal being, the true intentions and desires that move their hearts.

"The world" is the illusory realm of the cave, and "the light" is the sun, which can be known only by liberation from the cave. In the Gospel of Thomas, Jesus says, "I am the Light that is above them all. I am the All, the All came forth from me and the All attained to me. Cleave the wood, and I am there; lift up the stone and you will find me there" (logion 77). It is hard to give a definitive reading of this saying, but I would read it as saying that the world (the cosmos) came from the Light; it is, at its root, one with the Light; and it will return to the Light. The Light is present in all things as the true reality which underlies the appearances among which we think we live. If we pierce the veil of appearance, we will see the truth, which is Light and

Mind. Those who look for the kingdom seek the Light, and the Light is there; in Christ it draws near, making the veil almost transparent. And for those who have eyes to see, the veil is lifted, and the kingdom of Light is real and present.

Could the Jesus of the Synoptic Gospels have said or thought these things? At first it may seem not. Yet the presence of versions of Synoptic parables in Thomas suggests that there may be an underlying similarity between John's Gospel – from which some form of this saying could have come, though of course it did not – and the Synoptics. The similarity is hidden, and this may be why the parables are said to be "mysteries". They convey to those whose eyes are open what they do not explicitly say.

It is not too difficult, with John and Thomas before us, to say what that mystery may be. The Synoptics speak of the kingdom of God as something which is drawing near, as growing corn, as a great feast, as treasure, and as a vineyard to be cared for and to bear fruit. But the mystery, the secret teaching, is that it is Jesus, the one who speaks, who is the seed from which the corn grows, the bread and wine provided for the feast, the pearl beyond price, and the vine which is to bear fruit. What Jesus said, in rural Galilee and in a culture which tended to see the kingdom as a nationalist overthrow of Roman imperialism, held a much deeper meaning.

To see that meaning, we have to move beyond seeing Jesus as a Galilean holy man, and see him as one who was uniquely one with the eternal God. Some modern commentators are quite unable to imagine this, and so they have to see Jesus as a prophet who taught obedience to God and the *Torah*. They cannot imagine a young Jewish man as believing, much less knowing, that he was one with God.

There is no question that such a thought was liable to be regarded as blasphemy within traditional Judaism – though, according to the eminent Jewish scholar Jacob Neusner, there are rabbinic traditions which almost regard some great rabbinic teachers as embodiments (though not quite incarnations) of divine wisdom. Some scholars think of the Synoptic Gospels as presenting a Jesus who distanced himself from God ("Why do you call me good? No one is good but

God alone", Mark 10:18) and taught only that God's kingdom would come on earth in the near future. Then they see John's Gospel as a development which divinized Jesus and which would have shocked him deeply had he known about it.

We might, however, think of John and Thomas as expressing the belief that Jesus always regarded himself as one with God. But the Synoptics correctly report that he acted and spoke in parables and signs, revealing the truth of his unity with God in the metaphors and symbols of the Second Temple Judaism in which he was brought up. So Jesus could be heard as speaking of a future kingdom that God would inaugurate, and which he predicted. Yet John could interpret him as implying (or even, in John, as teaching) that the limits of traditional Jewish orthodoxy had been shattered, and that the divine and the human had been united in his person in a unique way, since he and his Father were "one". This would imply that Jesus inaugurated the kingdom of an interior union between divinity and humanity by his presence and action, though it was to develop in new ways that would have been unimaginable to his hearers.

If it was believed that Jesus was in some sense one with the divine, then it might well be said that all things came from him, were sustained in him, and would return to him — not to the human body and soul, but to the divine Word with which that body and soul were intimately and indissolubly united. The kingdom that in the Synoptics looks like a future society, perhaps ruled by Jesus, could then be seen by John as a present spiritual union which exists "in Christ", though it is to be fulfilled and completed for all the cosmos only at the end of time.

The existence of the Gospel of John and of the "secret" Gospels like that of Thomas suggests that belief in Jesus as the cosmic Word of God belongs to some quite early strands of Christianity. They are also evidence of a tendency towards forms of Gnosticism that the church rejected, because Gnosticism devalued the material world, even regarding it as the creation of an evil God. It made secret knowledge the means of salvation, instead of the love of God in Christ. And it tended to get lost in rather pointless speculations about divine emanations of various sorts.

The existence of the Synoptic Gospels suggests that Jesus
talked in simple ways that could be understood by a rural Galilean
population. He did not teach philosophy or abstract theology. But I
have argued that a study of the literary forms of speech used by Jesus
rules out a simple literal interpretation of his teaching. Spiritual
metaphor, symbolism, hyperbole, and prolepsis are central to his
forms of speech. They point towards, and are meant to evoke, a
veiled spiritual reality which is present but is to be fully unveiled in
an anticipated future.

We can see a tendency towards literalism within the New Testament
itself, especially in the early Pauline letters which look for an imminent
return of Jesus in glory, and also in early church literalizations of
ideas of heaven and hell. But such tendencies can be countered by
closer attention to the Old Testament use of symbolic language by
the prophets, and by the development of a rich sacramental theology,
a contemplative monastic spirituality, and the philosophically subtle
interpretations of the person of Jesus by the early church.

Early Christianity had to find a way between these Gnostic and
literalist tendencies, and it only did so by disputations and arguments
which were sometimes not entirely creditable. But the earliest
Synoptic Gospel, that of Mark, unambiguously presents Jesus as the
one who will come in glory to gather the elect (Mark 13:27), as one
who claims to be David's Lord, at God's right hand (Mark 12:37),
and as one who gives his life as a ransom for many (Mark 8:38).
This is not a picture of one who is just an apocalyptic prophet; it
is a picture of a Christ who mediates the divine life in an estranged
world, and who enacts in his own person a divine self-sacrifice which
liberates humans from estrangement and sin. This is a picture of a
God who enters into creation to reunite it to the divine life. If that
is so, then the teaching of Jesus will be the proclamation of this
most fundamental truth in the symbolic terms of Galilean messianic
expectation and longing for liberation, and especially in the extended
metaphors in narrative form which we call the parables. That points
to the possibility that John (and to some extent Thomas) has brought
out the fuller meaning of doctrines that are implicit and embryonic

in the Synoptic records of one who may seem at first to be little more than a Galilean holy man and healer.

Conclusion

I am primarily a philosopher, and one who has a natural inclination to idealism, to the view that the real basis of the physical cosmos and of human lives is one supreme Mind. I was trained in the tradition of linguistic analysis, so I take a great interest in the forms of language and the diverse sorts of things that language may convey. I have also been a teacher of Christian doctrine, and I have been mainly interested in the logical coherence and plausibility of traditional Christian formulations of belief in the historic creeds and in analysing in terms of modern thought the decisions of the early church (the first six or seven Ecumenical Councils).

It is these interests that I bring to bear on the analysis of the linguistic forms that Jesus is recorded in the Gospels to have used and on the metaphysical views that developed from early Christian faith. For knowledge of the Jewish and Hellenistic context of Jesus' thought and of the nature of the biblical texts, I have relied on the best scholarship known to me. I owe much to the groundbreaking work of New Testament scholars, both historians and experts in the languages and culture of the ancient Near East, some of whose books I have listed in the bibliography. Responsible scholarship must weigh very carefully the arguments given in these books, and I have tried to use their work in what I have written here.

The originality of this work, for what it is worth, lies in a fourfold thesis which is based primarily on analysis of the linguistic and conceptual forms attributed to Jesus by the Gospels. The thesis is that Jesus taught a gospel of conditional universal salvation, not a message of condemnation for all but a small "elect". Jesus' use of apocalyptic imagery was not literal, but was symbolic of a veiled spiritual teaching of the true nature and goal of creation as lying in liberation from egoism and in conscious union with God. His ethical teaching was one of mandating responsible autonomous moral decision-making, aimed at achieving human fulfilment in the light of conscious relationship to, imitation of, and participation in the being of a loving Creator.

This teaching implies a metaphysical view of the final union of divinity and humanity through a process of divine *kenosis* ("Here is the Lamb of God who takes away the sin of the world", John 1:29) and the apotheosis of the finite by its participation in the divine nature (the phrase is from 2 Peter 1:4, but John 14:20 entails it: "I am in my Father, and you in me").

There are many Christians who accept none of these interpretations of Jesus' teaching. What that shows is that the issue is not clear-cut and that much depends on the background beliefs that you bring to the reading of the texts, and on which elements of Jesus' teaching you find to be so basic that the whole body of texts must be interpreted in terms of them.

The first thesis is that God will make it possible for everyone to be saved (to come to know and love God for ever). This is sometimes called "conditional universalism". It does not claim that everyone will be saved. It claims that everyone *can* be saved, if at some time (even after earthly death) they repent and believe, and that we may hope and pray for that. It is worth noting that the two greatest Reformed theologians after Calvin, Friedrich Schleiermacher and Karl Barth, held this position, and that Pope John Paul II laid it out in his little book, *Crossing the Threshold of Hope.*[1] The view is based primarily on following out the implications of the claim that God is a God of unlimited self-giving love.

The second thesis is accepted in some form by most New Testament scholars, and notably by C.H. Dodd, who thinks that the apocalyptic symbols refer almost entirely to present political and spiritual realities; by Norman Perrin, who sees the symbols as untranslatable into non-symbolic terms; by Joachim Jeremias, who thinks of the eschatological statements as speaking of a kingdom which is "in the process of realization"; and by J.D. Crossan, who regards the apocalyptic material as not original to Jesus, and as referring to "the kingdom of the wise man", a present way of living, and not something that would happen in the future of the world. There is in America a widespread reaction against the more literal readings of Weiss and Schweitzer, and a greater scepticism about whether Jesus himself took apocalyptic imagery as central to his message. My own view is that these images point to Jesus' cosmic and divine status, which is indeed only to be fully revealed at the end of historical time, but which is presented by him in a symbolic, non-literal way.

The third thesis would be contested by those who find specific moral rules in the teaching of Jesus. But there are very few such rules. Gerd Theissen thinks there may be two: the prohibitions of remarriage and of oath-taking.[2] Most Christians do not take the prohibition on oath-taking as a literal command — many Christian ministers take an oath of loyalty when they are ordained! And different churches have different ways of qualifying a literal command that you should never end a relationship which you have promised to sustain until death — sometimes by simply not calling it "divorce", or by saying that you did not properly understand the promise. Such strategies seem to be ways of disobeying the real moral principle underlying the rule against divorce and remarriage while retaining a verbal obedience. I think it is more plausible to see Jesus' statements prohibiting oaths and divorce as similar to many of his other ethical statements in being hyperbolic figures of speech pointing to inner attitudes, not social rules. Jesus' general interpretation of the rules of the *Torah* reads them in a humane and life-enhancing way, stressing the dispositional mental attitudes that underlie them. I agree with Professor Sanders when he says, "This could eventually lead to the view that the law was unnecessary [for Gentiles], but it appears that Jesus himself did not draw this conclusion."[3] This thesis does not, of course, say that there are no moral rules. It says that we should work them out for ourselves in the light of acceptance of the love of God that is seen in Jesus. This is precisely the method of ethical reasoning that is used by Catholic moral theologians, usually known as "natural law" reasoning in ethics. It is what Jesus' method of teaching by asking questions, and what Jesus' life of forgiveness, of socializing with sinners, and of willingness to die for the redemption of the world, seem to me to imply.

The fourth thesis is one that German liberal theologians like Harnack derided as "mystical" or even superstitious. But it is a view that lies at the heart of Eastern Orthodox theology, and it has perhaps been neglected in Western Christianity mainly because of a desire to maintain the sovereignty and uniqueness of God over and against the finitude and sinfulness of men and women. That desire is laudable in itself. But it needs to be complemented by a recognition that in Christ humanity and divinity are truly united, that grace is always present in a sinful world, and that our living "in Christ" is an ontological truth. Karl Rahner, John Macquarrie, and Paul Tillich, each representing different modern Christian traditions, try to take account of this in their writings. Thus my claim that Christianity implies a form of idealism is not as radical or as threatening as it may seem.

The four theses, taken together, may seem to be propounding a new, more positive, more life-affirming, more science-friendly reading of Christianity. But in fact they are all deeply rooted in ancient Christian tradition and in some of the best modern biblical scholarship. If they seem new, it may be because what people think of as Christianity is often a Victorian invention of a rather authoritarian and judgmental God that has outlived its usefulness and lost its emotional purchase. If we tried to put the overall interpretation of Jesus' teaching that I have outlined in this book in more modern terms, we might get an outline of Christian faith something like this:

There is a God, a cosmic intelligence of supreme value, beauty, and wisdom. To know and relate to that God in full appreciation of its beauty and perfection, and to co-operate in realizing its creative and compassionate love, is the highest realization of the human virtues of sensitivity, understanding, creativity and empathy, the greatest fulfilment of positive human potentialities, and the greatest happiness attainable by human persons.

God has a purpose for the cosmos, which is for it to generate intelligent agents who may realize comprehension, compassion, creativity, contemplation, and community – a communion of being centred on the supremely good and beautiful.

God, however, necessarily expresses possibilities inherent in the divine being which unfurl their potentialities through emergent and dialectical interaction. God intends finite values, but their emergence necessarily realizes the possibility of evil and destruction as part of the self-expression of the divine. Thus human life is a battle of good and evil, in which good must overcome evil — by restraint but also always by love.

God will seek to transform that evil for good. But intelligent creatures are free to follow their own paths, the path of greed, hatred, and ignorance, or the path of non-attachment, compassion, and wisdom — the way of death or the way of life.

God acts to liberate humans from their condition, and Christians believe that Jesus, as presented in slightly different perspectives in the Gospels and early church letters, is the authentic image and act of God on this planet. He shows God's nature and purpose, and through him God acts to unite humans to the divine. What is conveyed in the Gospels is the character of God's nature and purpose, as seen in and through Jesus by very different people, who have filled in the details in personal and often imaginative ways.

The Spirit conveys the love and wisdom of God, as expressed in Jesus, to people throughout the world. The work of the Spirit is universal, and is not confined to any Christian church. But God does act effectively through word and sacraments in the churches, and the Spirit is rightly identified as the Spirit fully active in Jesus.

God wills that all intelligent beings should come to clear knowledge of and be filled with the dynamic love of God (that is salvation). God wills the loss of no one. God goes to the uttermost in self-giving to bring us to salvation (that is the meaning of the cross and of the resurrection).

The judgment is that we will realize the seriousness of our moral failures and blindness, and experience in ourselves to some extent and in some appropriate way the harm we have done to others. The point of such judgment is to bring us to contrition, and to an attempt to make recompense as far as we can for the ways in which we have hurt others. The gospel is that if we do that, and turn to God for his strength and love in our lives, God will forgive and empower us.

God stands ready to redeem all, but will not undermine human freedom. It is possible for humans to exclude themselves, by pride,

hatred, and greed, from the love of God. But God's purpose will
be fully realized in all who consent, though only in a world beyond
physical death, in a renewed and transfigured creation. God will not
destroy lives before everything has been done to save them, and will not
punish anyone endlessly or pointlessly. Thus the purpose of creation is
fulfilled in a loving community of many intelligent agents, expressing
values potential in the divine being, and guided by one Supreme Mind.
All evil will finally be destroyed, and God will bring all who respond
into the community of the Spirit. That will be the final flourishing of
the kingdom of God, when all creation is united in Christ, the eternal
spiritual reality through whom all things came into being.

Of course the historical Jesus did not say all this. But I believe that the
Jesus of the Synoptic Gospels uses metaphors, symbols, and parables
which are the seeds of such an understanding of God's nature and
purpose. That understanding had to be developed gradually as the
church came to see more fully its place in world history. We can see the
process beginning in John's Gospel, and being worked out in the great
Ecumenical Councils of the early church. In the modern world, it can
give rise to an even wider comprehension of God's purpose in this vast
cosmos when that purpose is seen as uniting all creation in the eternal
wisdom of God. God's purpose is the positive life-affirming purpose
of offering eternal life to all the creatures of time. God's purpose is
universal and God's love is unlimited. I believe that this is the heart of
Jesus' teaching and the heart of the Christian gospel. If that is so, then
it is good news indeed.

Notes

1 Approaching the Gospels

1. Crossan, *In Parables*, p. 4.
2. Borg and Wright, *The Meaning of Jesus: Two Visions*, pp. 82, 146.
3. *Dei Verbum* (Dogmatic Constitution on Divine Revelation), chapter 3, paragraph 2 in Austin Flannery, OP (ed.), *Vatican Council II: Vol. 1: The Conciliar and Postconciliar Documents,* new revised edition, Dublin: Dominican Publications, 1992.

2 Universal Salvation: The True Gospel

1. In *The Peaceable Kingdom*, Notre Dame, IN: University of Notre Dame Press, 1983.
2. Dodd, *The Parables of the Kingdom*, p. 14.
3. Dodd, *Parables of the Kingdom*, chapter 6.
4. Dodd, *Parables of the Kingdom*, p. 139.
5. Dodd, *Parables of the Kingdom*, p. 151.
6. Dodd, *Parables of the Kingdom*, p. 41.
7. Dodd, *Parables of the Kingdom*, p. 57.
8. Jeremias, *The Parables of Jesus*, p. 230.
9. Jeremias, *The Parables of Jesus*, p. 230, note 3.
10. Theissen and Merz, *The Historical Jesus*, p. 210.

3 The Cosmic Christ

1. Crossan, *In Parables*.
2. Crossan, *In Parables*, p. 64.
3. Crossan, *In Parables*, p. 35.
4. Jeremias, *The Parables of Jesus*, pp. 48 ff.

4 The Ethics of Personal Fulfilment

1. E.g. in *Jewish Law from Jesus to the Mishnah*, London: SCM Press, 1990.
2. Vermes, *Jesus the Jew*, p. 12.
3. Sanders, *The Historical Figure of Jesus*, p. 220.
4. Cf. Solomon, *Judaism and World Religion*, chapter 9.3.
5. Schleiermacher, *The Christian Faith*, First part, para. 32, p. 131.
6. Sanders, *The Historical Figure of Jesus*, pp. 210f.
7. Sanders, *The Historical Figure of Jesus*, p. 199.
8. Sanders, *The Historical Figure of Jesus*, p. 200.
9. Sanders, *The Historical Figure of Jesus*, p. 201.

5 Theosis: The Union of Human and Divine

1. Bauckham, *Jesus and the Eyewitnesses*, p. 411.
2. Sanders, *The Historical Figure of Jesus*, p. 71.
3. Lindars, *John*, p. 58.
4. In *The Community of the Beloved Disciple*, London: Chapman, 1979.
5. Lindars, *John*, p. 64.
6. Rahner, *The Trinity*, p. 22.
7. Plato, *The Republic* 7.14–21.

Conclusion

1. New York: Alfred A. Knopf, Inc., 1994.
2. Theissen, *The Historical Jesus*, p. 362.
3. Sanders, *The Historical Figure of Jesus*, p. 236.

Bibliography

Among previous books on Jesus and philosophy, two deserve special mention, both called *Jesus and Philosophy*, and published in 2009. One, edited by Paul Moser, and published by Cambridge University Press, is an edited collection of excellent articles by various theologians and philosophers. The other, by Don Cupitt, published by SCM Press, is a lively, challenging, and very readable book which adopts a radical view of Jesus as a teacher of secular ethics.

Books quoted in the text

Bauckham, Richard, *Jesus and the Eyewitnesses*, Grand Rapids, MI: Eerdmans, 2006.
Borg, Marcus and N.T. Wright, *The Meaning of Jesus: Two Visions*, New York: HarperCollins, 1999.
Brown, Raymond, *The Gospel According to John*, New York: Doubleday, 1966.
Crossan, John Dominic, *In Parables*, Sonoma, CA: Polebridge Press, 1992 (originally published 1973).
Dodd, C.H., *The Parables of the Kingdom*, London: James Nisbet, 1935 (quotes from revised edition, Fontana Books, 1965).
Jeremias, Joachim, *The Parables of Jesus*, 3rd revised edition, London: SCM Press, 1972.
Lindars, Barnabas, *John*, Sheffield: Sheffield Academic Press, 1990.
Macquarrie, John, *Principles of Christian Theology*, 2nd revised edition, London: SCM Press, 1966.
Sanders, E.P., *The Historical Figure of Jesus*, London: Allen Lane, Penguin, 1995.
Schleiermacher, Friedrich, *The Christian Faith*, Edinburgh: T. and T. Clark, 1989 (first published in German, 1830).
Solomon, Norman, *Judaism and World Religion*, London: Macmillan, 1991.
Theissen, Gerd and Annette Merz, *The Historical Jesus*, trans. John Bowden, London: SCM Press, 1998.
Vermes, Geza, *Jesus the Jew*, London: William Collins, 1973.

Books directly relevant to but not quoted in the text

Bultmann, Rudolf, *The Gospel of John*, Oxford: Blackwell, 1970 (English trans., 1941).
Bultmann, Rudolf, *Theology of the New Testament*, London: SCM Press, 1952–5.
Caird, G.B., *The Language and Imagery of the Bible*, London: Duckworth, 1980.
Crossan, J.D., *The Historical Jesus: The Life of a Mediterranean Jewish Peasant*, New York: HarperCollins, 1991.
Funk, Robert W., *The Gospel of Jesus, according to the Jesus Seminar*, Santa Rosa, CA: Polebridge Press, 1999.
Jülicher, Adolf, *Die Gleichnisreden Jesu*, Freiburg: J.C.B. Mohr, 1888–98.
MacIntyre, Alasdair, *After Virtue*, London: Duckworth, 1980.
Niebuhr, Reinhold, *The Nature and Destiny of Man*, vol. 2, New York: Scribner's, 1943.
Palmer, Humphrey, *How Parables Work*, Cardiff: Humphrey Palmer, 2008.
Pannenberg, Wolfhart, *Revelation in History*, London: Sheed & Ward, 1969.
Perrin, N., *Jesus and the Language of the Kingdom*, London: SCM Press, 1976.
Perrin, N., *The Kingdom of God in the Teaching of Jesus*, London: SCM Press, 1963.
Rahner, Karl, *The Trinity*, trans. Joseph Donceel, New York: Crossroad Herder, 1999.

Robinson, John, *In the End God*, London: SCM Press.
Schweitzer, Albert, *The Quest for the Historical Jesus: A Critical Study of its Progress from Reimarus to Wrede*, London: A. & C. Black, 1910 (originally published in German, 1906).
Thomas Aquinas, *Summa Theologiae*, 1a, 2–11, translated by Fathers of the English Dominican Province, New York: Benziger Bros, 1948.
Vermes, Geza, *Jesus and the World of Judaism*, London: SCM Press, 1983.
Via, D.O., *The Parables*, Philadelphia: Fortress Press, 1967.
Wright, N.T., *Jesus and the Victory of God: Christian Origins and the Question of God, Vol. 2*, London: SPCK and Minneapolis: Augsburg Fortress, 1996.
Zizioulas, John, *Being as Communion*, London: Darton, Longman, Todd, 1985.

Further reading

Further books by the author that explore the main themes of this book:

Conditional universalism and spiritual eschatology

What the Bible Really Teaches, London: SPCK and New York: Crossroad, 2004.
The Word of God?, London: SPCK, 2010.

Participative virtue ethics

Ethics and Christianity, Muirhead Library of Philosophy, London: Allen and Unwin, 1970 [esp. chapters 5 and 6].
The Rule of Love, London: Darton, Longman, Todd, 1989 [on the Sermon on the Mount]
The Divine Image, London: SPCK, 1976.
Religion and Human Fulfilment, London: SCM Press, 2008.

Unitive idealism

The God Conclusion, London: Darton, Longman, Todd, 2009.
More than Matter?, Oxford: Lion, 2010.

Index

Index   191